PRAISE
JAIMIE ENGLE
AND
JME BOOKS

L. Ron Hubbard Writers of the Future Award
Top Ten Book Kid Lit Reviews
Nebula, Bram Stoker & Shirley Jackson Nominee
Fl. Dept. of Education State Summer Reading List

"...the world Engle has created in this novel is an intriguing one, equal parts familiar and fantastic." *Kirkus Reviews*

"...belongs on your bookshelf - young or old - right along with Tolkien and Grimm." – *5 Star Amazon Review*

"I did not want to leave until the last page was turned." –*Kid Lit Reviews*

"...the same kind of universe you might meet Captain Malcolm Reynolds or Luke Skywalker in." –The Story Sanctuary Reviews

"Jaimie Engle brings "The Dredge" to an exciting, unexpected, and ultimately satisfying ending." –*Third Flatiron Editor*

BOOKS BY JAIMIE ENGLE

FICTION

Clifton Chase and the Arrow of Light (INtense Publications)
A boy is chosen to change the past by a magic arrow

Arrow of Light Coloring Book (INtense Publications)
Condensed coloring book adaptation of the novel

Clifton Chase on Castle Rock (INtense Publications)
Book two, adventures with Robin Hood

Castle Rock Coloring Book (INtense Publications)
Condensed coloring book adaptation of the novel book 2

The Dredge
Supernatural gifts are sought through deception in a future world

Dreadlands: Wolf Moon
A Viking boy must face shifting wolves or become their prey

The Toilet Papers: Places to Go, While you Go
A short-story collection to make the bathroom better

The Toilet Papers, Jr.
Short stories and poems for kids ages 8+

Metal Mouth
When lightning strikes, everything changes for Mahlorie.

NON-FICTION

How to Publish Your Book
A step-by-step guide to publish your book (#1Amazon New Release)

Clifton Chase and the Arrow of Light Teacher's Edition
Aligned Teacher's Edition to parallel the novel.

Visit the author at thewriteengle.com.

Write A **BOOK** THAT DOESN'T SUCK!

Indie Series
BOOK 2
A No Nonsense
Guide to
Writing Epic
Fiction

(Guaranteed to have ideas you've never heard before.)

JAIMIE ENGLE

Write a Book that Doesn't Suck

A No Nonsense Guide to Writing Epic Fiction

(Guaranteed Ideas You've Never Tried)

JME Books

Published in the United States by JME Books,
a division of The Write Engle, LLC,
P.O. Box 411242
Melbourne, FL 32941

Visit us on the Web: thewriteengle.com

For an author visit or bulk order discounts, visit us at jmebooks.com or email thewriteengle@gmail.com.

Summary: Writing techniques to write fiction novels.

ISBN-10: 1-7328786-5-X
ISBN-13: 978-1-7328786-5-5

10 9 8 7 6 5 4 3 2

JME Books

This is for anyone who ever wanted to write a great book but didn't know how.

JME Books

Introduction

I've been writing since I was seven, and most of it sucked. That's how we learn though, writing badly so we can figure out how to write well. Over the years of writing conferences, reading books on crafts, mentoring, and finally editing other books that sucked, I discovered patterns and mistakes all newbie authors tend to follow for one reason or another.

This book will give writing techniques that go well beyond the scope of setting, character, and plot. I guarantee most of what you'll read you've never thought of before. And don't worry. I reference tons of contemporary and classic books and films to help you along the way.

Now, let's get started and write that book that doesn't suck!

Chapter One:

The Order of the World

Our world is the setting for the drama of our lives. We have sky above, earth beneath, and water all around. Animals and insects populate these spaces, with jobs to help maintain the homeostasis of our existence. Outside the atmosphere, the universe goes on without borders, a place that doesn't influence our day to day affairs, but a part of our world. Other people fill in our stories to provide relationships, friendships, villainy, and as background noise.

Our world, our universe, is the setting—a perfect place, populated with amazing creatures and main characters, who misbehave when antagonists bring conflict into the story world, then fight before Evil gains control of the realm forever.

Timeless tales weave this powerful human truth throughout their plots.

Superman.

It's A Wonderful Life.

Hunger Games.

World building is a crucial element of your story. It is bigger than setting and it can even be part of characterization. There are several steps to include when building your universe. First and foremost, you must establish a clear time and place for your story to take place. The story world law is foundational. The order of life is stated. And the characters aren't introduced until this world is complete.

As a writer, it is critical that your reader quickly understand the story world. When and where does the story take place? If it's speculative fiction, what are the rules or lore of this world? If it's historical, what changes alter or prohibit the characters from making the same choices you would? Many authors begin with dialogue or story problem too quickly, and the reader gets lost, not yet grounded in the story world.

Check out the first paragraph of *The Hunger Games* by Suzanne Collins from Scholastic Books. What does the beginning tell us?

- The family is poor because this character shares a bed with a sibling
- Rough canvas and mattress imply a time long ago, a post-apocalyptic / dystopian future, or a different world altogether
- Wherever this is, it's a scary, unstable world for this little girl to have recurring nightmares
- Dad's either dead or gone because she climbed

in with 'our mother', not 'our parents'

- The Day of the Reaping is not in the past of our timeline or our world

Reaping literally means "to harvest the crop" (Merriam Webster Dictionary). The only crop reaping capable of inducing nightmares would be human or animal, because not too many people get scared about picking apples. This indicates a dystopian future since the Day of the Reaping doesn't exist.

The world is clearly established in the first paragraph. Not completely, but enough for me to follow. I know where this story starts, when in the timeline of history, who the people are, and the mood and tone are both set. This is so important for your reader to know as soon as possible.

Your world begins as an empty page, unformed, that you will populate with characters so real, your reader will breathe life into them. To see the new world, you will need light and darkness. Day and night.

Time is a crucial component of your story world. When does your story take place? Past, present, future? Day, night? Winter, summer? These decisions affect the plot, problems, and solutions, while providing additional story threads. Take a story from the past and set it in the future to see how it plays out. Take a scene in the summer and set it in the winter and watch the new problems your characters face.

Boundaries are the edges of the world you've crafted. They set the stage for what the reader will experience through the pages of your book. But your world shouldn't end there. It doesn't end there. The implication that this stage existed before your story started and will continue after your story ends is crucial to building a believable universe.

Does your universe have clearly marked boundaries for your reader? Is it the size of a bedroom or beyond the known universe? You must answer these questions before you begin.

The next consideration is the actual setting. Where does your story take place? Are the locations clearly marked for your reader? Is it a place the reader probably knows? This will determine how much detail is needed. If it's a place you have invented, like a fantasy or science fiction world, you will need to give your reader lots of details to establish it, even down to the way it runs: government, currency, life and death, religion, trade, etc. If it's historical, you will need some of these elements for accuracy (and please be accurate) but you won't need to explain quite as much.

Now, give your reader a peek into the sun and moon, the stars, the universe beyond your world. Your story needs to appear larger than where the narrative takes place. Your reader may never see beyond the world you create, but they must believe the map keeps growing beyond your story's borders.

The setting is now complete. A world exists. A universe grows beyond the story. The world is self-sustained. Now what? Now, it's time to populate and set up a hierarchy of order.

Main characters are important. They tell your story, show it. However, this book isn't about those storytelling techniques you already know. It's about the ones you've never thought of before. So, let's focus on the other characters, the ones in the background, who bring credibility to your scenes. The extras. The characters who exist in your story world to make it more believable, but don't move the story forward.

In *Hunger Games*, that would be the Peacemakers, the merchants in the Hob, and the miners. They are part of District 12, but they aren't for whom the story takes place.

Does your story have filler characters or entities that live in your story world, but don't necessarily drive the plot? It needs to.

Next, you need to separate these fillers into levels of importance. Some provide food, shelter, or clothing for the community. Some are your hero's companions. Others govern the land so the heroine can grow crops. They fertilize the soil. They plow the fields. They pick up the trash. They are integral to your character's existence.

Do you have elements in your story world that keep your society functioning? Is there a believable hierarchy in your story world?

Finally, you have the stage set. You are ready to introduce the main characters. This person or persons, monster or alien, will be given charge over the story world, even if they aren't the "one in charge." They will take care of this incredible universe you've invented, while keeping its inhabitants safe. They are a piece of you, the good guy, the bad guy, and the benevolent others, created in your image. After all, you are the god of your story world. You have provided the ideal environment for your characters to thrive in. But beware. There is a serpent with other plans slithering through your story, waiting for the perfect moment to strike.

Define your story world by genre, time/year, season, day or night and setting:

_____

_____

_____

_____ .

Name at least three filler characters that will be part of your story world or the opening scenes for building the world.

_____

_____

_____ .

What lies outside your story world? Your universe's edge?

_____

_____

_____

_____ .

What sort of hierarchy can you create between some of the groups within your world? Where does your hero fit?

_____

_____

_____ .

Pick a story with a great world or universe. What stands out the most? How can you emulate that in your own book?

_____

_____

_____ .

Chapter Two:

The Villain and the Vixen

When does the villain show up in the story? When everything seems perfect. When the love interest comes along. In pacing your story, it is the moment where the reader pauses to catch their breath. They revel in the beauty and perfection of your story world, like Dorothy landing in Oz. But the wicked witch lurks in the shadows waiting to strike, waiting for the right character to enter the scene, to release chaos into the perfect world.

Our job as writers is to breathe life into our characters, not to mold them from clay. They need to be complex, realistic entities with a spirit and a soul, not just a body.

What makes us human?

What separates us from animals?

- Humor
- Appreciation of beauty
- Self-consciousness
- Awareness of death
- Understanding time
- Meaning of life
- Malleability
- Lack of harmony with nature
- A sense of morality
- Character
- Free moral agency
- Capacity for wisdom
- Desire to worship
- Love

If your characters don't exhibit varying degrees of these traits, they are animals wearing human skin. This skill takes time to cultivate, but by reading books and observing what makes a character great, you will soon develop it. I like to study actors when I watch films to see the dynamics of their flaws. To me, it helps me translate these inconsistencies into my own work.

A great many stories present the main character with choices through objects, which in and of themselves are harmless. They are neutral, like the red and blue pills in *The Matrix*, but their consequences are not. In your stories, you need to have "things" that tempt your characters to act. They must dangle as lures that desensitize them by becoming a familiar place within the story world and therefore less ominous. ("My precious...")

Your main character should have the willpower to face his task and not be easily swayed. He must do what he was created to do, day in and day out. That's when you throw in the wrench. Amidst all the perfection and beauty you've crafted in your hero's story, he will become lonely. He has no one to share it with, no one to enjoy the journey and grow with.

Enter the love interest.

Lois Lane.

Rhett Butler.

Juliet.

The love interest brings out the main character's weaknesses and can either be oblivious to their impact or diabolical in their strategy. Their role is to play helper and fill in something missing in the main character. This doesn't mean your book must mirror the *50 Shades*; it's more of a "you complete me" *Jerry Maguire* thing.

Take some time to dissect and list the pluses and minuses, the positive and negative traits, between the main character and the love interest in your favorite stories. Together, they probably form a perfect ten. For example, where one is a two for shyness, the other is an eight in outgoing. Where one is a three for compassion, the other is a seven for tolerance.

Build these traits into your characters and flip them in the love interest. You'll provide both deep-felt connections and hostile contradictions within their relationship, which makes for believability and, more importantly, relatable characters for your reader. And don't forget to make some things they both have in common. They need something to talk about, right?

What comes next to spoil this perfect story?

Enter the villain, stage right.

Ironically, you will create a nemesis whose sole purpose is to destroy the perfect world and incredible hero you've written. Seems a bit counterproductive, doesn't it? Remember, whether you like it or not, your villain reflects you, of your upbringing, prejudices, biases, and experiences, if only the flipside.

When I craft villains, I ask myself, "What *wouldn't* I do in this situation?" or "What could this character do that would be the most horrific thing imaginable?" These answers are based in my beliefs and convictions, then left for the antagonist to answer.

The best villain twists the story rules enough to harbor doubt, then sits back to watch what happens. Why does this work? Because a partial truth is always easier to believe than a flat out lie. Your characters are smart. Your readers are smarter. The partial truth— *"This is just a game, Ender"*—is easier to swallow.

We want to believe it's the whole truth so badly that we override our common sense to satisfy it. That's human nature. Partial truths work because people want to hear the answer that supports their opinions or desires. They don't necessarily want the whole truth, but rather a diluted version that gives them the okay to proceed with their heart's desire.

And we all know how reliable the heart can be. Again, the questions from *The Matrix* rings true: the red or the blue pill?

This form of deception is seen in Frodo's quest in *Lord of the Rings* and Harry Potter's journey to defeat Lord Voldemort. Both Frodo and Harry are fed just enough of the truth to hook them and bring them to the dark truth of their journey.

What point in your story would have the most impact on the hero's journey for the love interest to enter?

_____

_____

_____ .

How much alike and different are they? Do they fight too much, not enough? Get along? Get along too much? Can you make them complimentary?

_____

_____

_____ .

What is the perfect time to introduce the villain?

_____

_____

_____ .

What half-truth does the hero choose to believe that harms his relationship with the vixen?

_____

_____

_____ .

How can you make the villain more human?

_____

_____

_____ .

Chapter Three:

Conflict

Conflict is inevitable. It's not always bad. In fact, it can be quite good. Conflict builds tension, creates engagement, and pushes the story forward. It forces characters to grow or to stand their ground. Conflict is sometimes confused with bullying, because believe it or not, a lot of people don't like to be told they're wrong. I know… who knew?

Conflict in nature forms canyons. Sand rubs against rock for countless years until it carves through, changing the appearance of the stone as it builds new formations. Without this chiseling away of the rock, the beauty within would remain hidden. The same is true of inner conflict and conflict between characters.

As your story world is altered by conflict, change is inevitable. The rules of Kansas don't apply in Oz. Muggles adhere to different boundaries and limitations than do witches and wizards inside

Hogwarts. And the rules in Narnia are completely different than those in World War II England. It is a subtle, yet key element between a story that works and one you can't put down.

But rules are made to be broken.

In your story world, the clearer the rules, the easier they will be to break. Having either an antagonist or protagonist break them will naturally result in conflict erupting between the two, and beyond to the other characters and communities in your novel.

Look at the story rules, and how they are handled by the protagonist and antagonist, of several of your favorite books. By breaking the rules, what emotions rise to the top and what conflict does this create?

Now, look at your own story. Are your story rules clearly established? How can the protagonist or antagonist break them and to what affect? What emotions result from these choices? And how can you use those emotions to escalate tension in the story?

In *Jumanji* by Chris van Allsburg, the town changes every time the dice is thrown. With each additional conflict, the character's emotional stakes raise. The characters must grow and evolve to handle each new story problem. This can be seen in van Allsbug's other book *Zathura*. Like *Jumanji*, this board game alters the world with each new spin, adding to the tension as the conflict grows. But the consequences of each spin can't be erased, not until the game is finished.

Each board game brings out the true conflict in its story. It's not the game or the crazy creatures that come out it. It's a boy forgotten by his family and a girl who doesn't want to be called crazy. It's a kid who feels invisible and another who wants to be unseen. These inner-relational issues bubble up to the surface after enough exterior conflict push them out. Does your story do that? It should, and it could with a few tweaks.

Think of it this way, if your story world and its inhabitants look the same on the first page as they do on the last page, you may need to clarify the rules of your story world. Then, find ways that either the antagonist or protagonist can break them, upping the tension and resulting in an altered story world for the characters to figure out.

In my book *Exposure*, a boy loses his parents and finds a roll of film buried in a drawer in his new caretaker's home. When he goes to the only place in town that can develop it, he discovers he's stuck there unless he can solve the clues hidden within the photographs. Each image builds the tension and conflict within this world he finds himself a part of. And at his center, he is desperate to prove his parents are still alive, believing the film holds all the answers. What he finds are broken rules and more conflict than he can handle.

The plot of brother against brother is a conflict pressure cooker. I mean, who doesn't love a little sibling rivalry? *Supernatural* has built a franchise on the ups and downs of this relationship. We have followed Sam and Dean for years as they navigate through a life of conflict and change, particularly over their varying view of their parents. The need to be accepted by family, especially by parents, is in all of us. Some people spend their whole lives seeking this approval and never find it, even after their parents are dead. Through the wrong lens, this favoritism can easily cause one sibling to detest the other, or to find their parents alive one day due to strategic moves by angels and demons. If the shoe fits...

The Dursleys in *Harry Potter* favor Dudley in a grotesque display. Luke Skywalker learns Darth Vader is his father and faces a serious choice that raises tension in the story. The characters in *Holes* all have mommy and daddy issues.

The Lemonade War.

Cinder.

Beezus and Ramona.

All these stories take the timeless tool of sibling rivalry, with the right twist, to create conflict and change. Utilizing the human need to be accepted by one's parents, sprinkled with favoritism and sibling rivalry, you can create intense story problems and consequences between your characters.

And now that the rules have been broken, your story will flow like clockwork!

How have you created a unique story world where rules change with conflict?

_____

_____

_____ .

Name 3-5 of your clearly established story rules.

_____

_____

_____ .

How can the protagonist or antagonist break them?

_____

_____

_____ .

What conflict results from these choices?

_____

_____

_____ .

How can you use those choices to escalate tension in the story?

_____

_____

_____ .

Chapter Four:

The Hero

The hero's plight connects us to one another. We can see our own strengths and weaknesses played out through the hero's choices and shortcomings. Who doesn't want to know that somewhere, someone has it all under control, and if we need help, help is on its way?

"It's a bird, it's a plane, no, it's Superman!"

Sometimes, though, it's not that simple. Here you are, going along in your story world, with great characters and story twists. When suddenly, you realize that the story has gone in its own direction, as if its own entity without your assistance.

It's like a rebellious teenager. What do you do? How can you fix it?

Many times, you feel you can't, and the delete button calls to you. Or if you write freehand, like I do, the paper shredder taunts of its insatiable hunger. You could drawer the book, but even then, you know the story is no longer your own, having been hijacked by your characters. And just when all seems lost, one character won't stop talking to you, won't get out of your head.

"I can fix this," it whispers.

And you know at that moment, a hero has been born.

The corrupt world is an awesome opportunity to have a hero rise from the ashes. It's what pushes Katniss Everdeen and Harry Potter and Bruce Wayne and Clark Kent. Justice. The people are weak, sheltered, or afraid of those who hold power over them. An imbalance in the force. Someone needs to tip the scales for the greater good.

What elements of oppression and despair have you built into your story world and characters? Can you kick it up a notch or layer it on a grander scale, so it isn't only about a boy who loses his parents, but also about a city that has lost all hope?

In *Ender's Game*, Ender Wiggin commands a fleet to destroy an 'evil' alien planet by wiping it off the map. His crew follows his revolutionary orders, while Ender's commanders watch in awe. They all trust him, both those who think it's a game and those who know better.

The hero leads to victory. He doesn't question his orders. He doesn't try to please anyone but his own innate gut. And he never stops short of ultimate victory. Game over. The stakes are on the hero's shoulders. All failures are ultimately his.

What elements can you throw into your story to greaten the hero's plight? Changing the rules is precarious, because there still needs to be a strong level of believability or else you risk losing your reader. But done correctly, the tension and stakes rise dramatically, drawing your character from the crowd to the hero's circle.

The other story element that helps with this sort of tension and rising stakes is the ticking time bomb. Time is set and will eventually run out. The thriller. If you can utilize time as a threat, it always boosts the hero's journey. She must make hard, split-second decisions. She must stay focused at all costs. She must reach the climax before time runs out. So many stories incorporate this device.

Perhaps the most well-known is Cinderella. "You have till midnight." This puts not only a cost on the magic, but pressure on the lowly stepdaughter to become the hero of her own adventure. Shrek, too, uses the time bomb in the first film, with Fiona one way by day, and another by night. So does Ariel and Aurora. It's a very effective tool to build tension and lead the reader on a clear map to a certain goal. Beat time and win, run out of time and lose.

Not in all cases, but in many situations, the distance between the social status of the hero and the actual result of becoming a hero is directly proportionate to the success of the story. Do you like how I made up a formula using math words? Me too. In all seriousness, if you can have someone who is extremely unlikely become the hero, it is much more impressive than the tall, dark, and handsome guy or gal saving the day. It's part of the reason why the comic book heroes take on non-hero personas in their "normal world." Clark Kent is a goober. Bruce Wayne is a narcissist. It works because that's not who they are. It's the opposite of who they are.

On the other end of the spectrum, take a guy like Shrek. He is the perfect hero because he is so not a hero! The hero is in him, much in the same way the ogre is in Fiona. Together, they find who they are and become even more, which is why it's one of the best movies ever, and that's not my opinion. Okay, fine. It is my opinion, but I'm sure you agree.

Marrok from my novella *The Dredge* is from the lowest level of his society. He never actually reaches much higher than that, as far as status goes. What he finds instead is his place, his role in his world, which includes becoming the sacrifice he was prophesied to become.

There are many ways your character can become a hero. It's up to you to give them the right environment and let them discover their purpose as they help you write the plot.

Speaking of which, anytime you can craft an environment and plot that go against the grain, you are in a good spot. Let it lead to a decision that has a life or death outcome by a certain time, and you will guarantee the rise of a hero.

What elements can you throw into your story to greaten the hero's plight?

_____
_____
_____ .

Did your main character start off low enough to grow? Name some of the plot points of growth.

_____
_____
_____ .

How can you include the ticking time bomb? Life or death stakes? Give 3-5 for each.

_____
_____
_____ .

Name your favorite hero. What makes them great?

_____
_____
_____ .

In what ways can you show some of these characteristics in your own hero?

_____
_____
_____ .

Chapter Five:

Let it Rain!

As a good parent, you want what's best for your children. You want to help when you can, wipe their tears, and make their road through life as easy as possible. As the creator of your characters, this type of treatment makes for extremely boring literature. The more problems and chaos and rain you can throw at your characters, the better! As Stephen King puts it, throw characters into a difficult situation and watch them squirm their way out.

As your story god, you can't make it easy for your characters when they face consequences. You can't reach down and scoop them up as the floods come. No, quite the contrary. You must raise the flood water so high that the mountaintops are covered, leaving your characters riding the swells, praying they'll make it out alive. You cannot lower the stakes. That's where the story is! That's where your character's true colors show, like in real life.

You must make it rain.

In the *Wizard of Oz*, Glenda visits Dorothy in Munchkinland. What if she had flown her to the Emerald City and the Wizard had sent her home immediately? Better still, what if she had clicked her heels together three times the moment she stepped into the ruby slippers? Dorothy would have gone back home to her same disappointments and troubles. She wouldn't have learned any lessons and would have repeated her mistakes.

By having her face the Wicked Witch of the West, help her new friends grow, and watch her only ride float off, all the while thinking Auntie Em had died or given up hope, Dorothy's heart changes. She regrets running away. She regrets wanting to leave home. She realizes that everything she needs is in her own backyard. After all, there's no place like home.

I took a class with Orson Scott Card once. He said that when he writes, he never uses his first idea to get his characters out of a tough situation. It's usually the easiest to come up with and doesn't require much from the characters. He suggested coming up with three to five more ideas per scene in which there is major tension or plotting.

The next book I wrote after taking his class was much different than the rest. In one scene of *Metal Mouth*, the main character Mahlorie runs through the woods, in the middle of a storm, headed to a house she's never been to before. Following Card's suggestion, I threw a tree in her path, one she couldn't climb or go around. She was forced into the water, during torrential downpours and intense lightning. But that wasn't enough. My next idea was a gator. It sat on the opposite shore, slid into the water, and headed toward her. Her goal was to swim faster than the gator could to reach the shore and the safety of the house. It ended up as one of the most intense scenes I've ever written, and it's because I let it rain. Literally.

Pain is needed to change, and your hero needs pain. You can't be a helicopter parent of a hero. It doesn't work that way. Think about the loss Frodo faces to become a hero. He is in physical pain, mental anguish, betrayed by friends, abandoned by family, and ultimately, he never gets to go back home, the one place he cared about and the only thing that kept him going on his journey.

Eleven from *Stranger Things* is a bouquet of pain. Imagine if her father had been kind. Or if the Upside Down had been easy to defeat. She is the reason the darkness is in our world to begin with, and it's a huge weight she bears throughout the seasons. It pushes her away from her friends in search of a family she thinks she needs, leaving them in harm's way. She finally comes to terms with the fact that she is the only one who can protect her friends, who are more her family than anything else.

What if things had been easier for her? What if the burden had been shared by another character? Would she have grown to become the hero we love? Doubtful.

Have you rescued your hero instead of letting him face the consequences of his choices? Lessons can't be learned when there is nothing at stake to lose. This is true of our characters too. They must face consequences, without our intervention as authors. Dumbledore knew this, and it's why Harry became our hero. If Dumbledore had stepped in at any time then Harry never would have completed his hero's journey and Voldemort, in some small way, would have won.

Have you made it too easy for your hero to succeed? Where can you make it rain? What crutch could you take away that would raise the floodwaters? Let the hero rescue the day, but not until after she slays a dragon or two.

Have you rescued your hero instead of letting him face the consequences of his choices?

_____

_____

_____ .

Where have you made it easy for your hero to succeed?

_____

_____

_____ .

Find a scene in your story that you can rework. Come up with 3-5 additional problems to add in.

_____

_____

_____ .

Are there places where you went with a cliché solution to a problem in your story? Brainstorm a few options and go with the third or fourth one.

_____

_____

_____ .

Chapter Six:

The Magic of Three

Have you ever noticed jokes are delivered in threes? First guy does something, second guy does something even bigger, third guy delivers the punch line. Or that one knock-knock joke about a banana and an orange, where you really are glad by the third knock that he didn't say banana.

"Two's company; three's a crowd."

"Three strikes, you're out!"

"Three-two-one-blast off!"

What's the point?

By setting story up this way, it adds to the believability and the tension in the build. Three holds a cadence in our psyche.

Three Little Pigs.

Goldilocks and the Three Bears.

The Three Billy Goats Gruff.

Threes hold power in writing and in life.

Beginning, middle, end.

Sky, land, sea.

Child, adult, senior.

The first time we see something in a story, it's eye catching.

Gandolph is in the first scenes of *The Lord of the Rings.*

The second time, it's important.

He disappears, then returns with new information.

The third time, it's impactful.

His last good-bye makes us wonder if we'll ever see him again, which we do in the final battle, as he helps save the day.

Rumpelstiltskin allows for three guesses of his name.

Goldilocks sits in three chairs, eats three bowls of porridge, and sleeps in three beds before being confronted by three bears. We remember these elements in threes.

In sentence structure, repetition in threes builds power.

"I came. I saw. I conquered."

It also works in pacing when you are speeding up or slowing down a scene by using three sentences that either go up or down in word count to make a point like this: 4-3-2 or 3-4-5. Here's an example of both:

She fought him off. Her hand slipped. He won. (4-3-2)

The dog barked. The girl didn't care. The two became best friends. (3-4-5)

A series of three parallel words, known as

tricolons, are fun to write, fun to read, and fun to share... see how I worked that in? The cadence and almost poetic aspect of adding these elements into your writing is not difficult. It requires earnest attention in editing, because most of us aren't going to stop the story to craft some literary device.

If you take time to read story and movie reviews by critics—you know those ones they use in the trailers or put on the back of books—you'll notice the magic of threes in use.

"Powerful. Inciteful. Original."

"This book will leave you breathless, panting, and wanting more."

Okay, so maybe those suck, but you get the point. Do some research and find a few on your own.

Even the story structure of 'boy meets girl, boy loses girl, boy gets girl back', follows the rule of threes.

The problem comes when you force the threes, making your writing sound mechanical and formulaic, inorganic in much the same way as someone who is bad at telling jokes misses the punchline.

Where have you used the magic of threes naturally in your story? Can you bring that out more to connect with your reader?

Let's really look at the power of threes in structure. In the first act, the exposition establishes the main characters and their relationships to the world around them. We are introduced to our protagonist who is forced into Act II through an inciting incident and the point of no return. Three elements: establish, incite, and turning point.

Act II is where the bulk of the story takes place, but without an inciting incident, you and your reader will never arrive here. This should be the longest part of the story and include organic elements of the power of threes. It is separated equally by the halfway point. The first half of the act is the fun and games, the testing, trying, and discovery in a safe way. Try-fail, try-fail, try-false victory or try-false defeat. Think of the superhero figuring out his powers before the bad guy shows up.

The second half is when everything goes wrong. The bad guys close in. All is lost. The dark night of the soul ensues. More threes.

Act III concludes the story with climax, falling action, and resolution. Again, three distinct movements that define this section of a story. Do you have a clear opening and closing to the three acts of your narrative? There should be a definitive set up period, confrontation section, and a final resolution.

Magic of threes are all throughout the story, define the story, and build the story. They are contained in the very sentence structure and elements of writing the story. Try-fail, try-fail, try-succeed. Now *that's* the magic of threes!

Where have you used the magic of threes naturally in your storyline?

_____
_____
_____ .

Write some sentences you can enhance with the magic of threes.

_____
_____
_____ .

Name what begins and ends your Act I, Act II, and Act III moments. If you don't know, then they aren't clear to the reader either.

_____
_____
_____
_____
_____
_____
_____
_____
_____ .

Chapter Seven:

Foreshadow Through Character

Foreshadow is a powerful tool. Small incidents can become huge connections later in the story through plot, character, or both. Parallel events layer your novel with expectations that your reader will pick up on. They allow your story to grow beyond a surface relationship into something so powerful that it becomes a classic.

Holes by Louis Sachar brilliantly works through the parallel of past and present with Kissing Kate and the "no-good-dirty-rotten-pig-stealing-great-great-grandfather." Stanley didn't know he was fulling his grandfather's debt owed to Madame Zeroni when he carried Zero up the mountain. That one event brought forth the onions, which enabled his dad to finally find something to quench the stench in shoes, and they discovered the missing money that all the boy's blindly dug holes to find. It was a truly brilliant way to incorporate foreshadow through double narrative.

Star Wars foreshadows Luke flirting with the Dark Side, following in his father's footsteps, only to break out, not only himself, but Anakin in the end. Both Darth Vadar and Luke lose their hand. They both are seduced by Palpatine. They both have great power and are destined to bring balance to the universe. Only one chooses the forces of good and the other of evil. Luke and Leah together balance Anakin's choices, and foreshadowing brings layer upon layer of story for us to fall in love with.

My novel *Dreadlands* utilizes foreshadowing, so much so, that I discovered half of it as I wrote the book. For example, in the first scene, Arud shoots and kills a deer. In that moment, I knew (half-spoiler alert) that someone very important to him was going to die, and this moment foreshadowed that death. In edits, I went back to the scene with the deer and really drew out the moment, showing the boy's gratitude to the animal for its blood sacrifice so that he might live.

"The sins of the father" is a powerful foreshadow tool. Generational curses or repeating the mistakes of the family, create great tension as your character battles between his fate and trying to change it. Redemption tastes that much sweeter when your character manages to break the family curse and create a new path for the next generation.

In some stories, like *Hunger Games*, the characters pay for the sins of the father in a world they didn't do anything to corrupt. They are forced into a society that dictates their present and future based off a past they had nothing to do with.

Ender pays for the sins of the father by living in a world fearful of future attacks by an alien race. This Formic race nearly extinguished life on earth years earlier, and while they've never returned, the fathers haven't forgotten. Ender incurs the debt from the sins of the world before him as he annihilates, through genocide, the Formics. Card's book *The First Formic War* shows the original sins of the father that Ender now pays for.

The *Back to the Future* trilogy is riddled with the use of foreshadow and the sins of the father. The diner and clock tower and head bumps are common ground that the parallel universes share. Marty McFly alters his father's life by going back in time, therefore altering his own. But then, in the third movie (magic of threes for sure!), he meets a relative he didn't know he had and is able to change his own past, or future, or whatever. It's my favorite series of all time. If I could only watch one film series over and over forever, this would be it.

What similarities can you draw between your character's journey and plot points throughout your story? How can you accentuate those choices to impact the plot even greater?

In Stephen King's book *On Writing* he mentions the thread of blood that appeared in his novel *Carrie*. He hadn't intended to, but there was blood present at every major plot point in the book. By editing the accidental coincidences and turning them into purposed foreshadow, *Carrie* launched his career and became a story that resonates with readers' years after they finish reading it.

Utilize what's already in your story to make connections and foreshadows that will impact your reader. You might be surprised to find what you've organically built into the story. Take those loose threads and tie them together to create layers that deepen your theme, plot, and relationship with your reader. And don't be afraid to leave some of them loose, in case you have ideas for sequels.

Choose one coincidence in your story that could you foreshadow and summarize it here.

_____
_____
_____ .

In what ways could you incorporate the sins of the father's being paid by the sons in your plot?

_____
_____
_____ .

Have you deliberately created foreshadowing but never come back to develop it? Try now.

_____
_____
_____ .

Does your story leave room for developing into or from a foreshadowed moment, like Ender's Game with the First Formic Wars? Consider a few plot points you can work from here.

_____
_____
_____
_____
_____ .

Chapter Eight:

Tension and Strife

Imagine if your uncle suddenly lost his job and moved his family into your home. Uncle helps Dad straighten out the garage, where he sets up a cot and creates a man cave. Auntie helps Mom in the garden by day and has a happy home in the spare bedroom (office) by night. And that no-good kid of theirs doesn't do anything, except make a mess that you get blamed for, play video games, and oh yeah, share your room. Suddenly, your trophies have been displaced, your clothes wedged into one drawer, and there's a hand towel rolled up on the floor for your new bed.

And the fighting ensues.

You are on edge, waiting for your turn in the bathroom, trying to steal back your bed, and hurrying to get the last piece of bacon so at least you can say you had one.

What happened?

Your home used to be so peaceful, and according to the conversations you've overheard between Dad and Uncle, your cousin has never been confrontational before. Really? Tell that to the big welt on the back of your thigh.

The problem is there's not enough room for two families to live under the same roof. This setup is a guarantee for strife, with two ways of doing things, two sets of rules, multiple expectations, space constraints, and clashing personalities.

In Bill Allen's book *Orson Buggy's The Big Fang Theory* the bully's mom marries Orson's dad, and they not only move-in together, but the boys must share a bedroom. What a mess! Privacy is gone and Orson fears for his life. No matter how hard everyone tries, tension and strife escalate. And you know how easily people get riled up when they are part of a group mentality. Look at *Lord of the Flies* or *Hunger Games* or *Maze Runner* for proof.

There are two great writing truths derived from this scenario. First, get your people in the same place in need of the same things and strife will follow.

Goldilocks and the Three Bears.

Divergent.

Rita Hayworth and the Shawshank Redemption.

If characters are forced to share a car or a tent or one of them loses everything and is forced to rely on the other (*The Life of Pi*), you will provide organic opportunity for them to react to the world around them. Want to see who's inside someone's skin?

Make them uncomfortable, and then take away their security and control. You'll see the true hearts of your characters, and it may not be so pretty.

The other truth is the idea of placing beauty within walking distance danger. By creating settings where the two attempt to coexist, you will evoke strong emotions from your readers. Don't believe me? Try these images: The beauty of Oz in full Technicolor and then BAM! Black smoke shattered by the presence of the Wicked Witch of the West. Or Hobbits and dwarves and elves (oh my!) in Rivendell, then BAM! Vile Orcs, broken bodies, and bloodied rivers. Or what about Pinocchio heading off to Pleasure Island?

Beauty + Evil = Fear.

Plain and simple.

Find places in your book to add fear and strife through contradictory settings and heart-breaking scenes. Put unlikely characters close, then force them closer. Take everything away that makes them comfortable and then stand back and watch. Tension and strife are bound to happen. Just be close by, ready to write them out of it, at the very last possible moment.

Name 3-5 places you can add tension and strife to your book. Choose a scene or two and work out.

_____
_____
_____ .

What comforts can you take away from your characters?

_____
_____
_____ .

How can you squeeze unlikely or unfriendly characters together even tighter than you already have?

_____
_____
_____ .

Do you have places in your book where you can show bad close to beauty in order to build strife?

_____
_____
_____ .

Chapter Nine:

Back-story and Clichés

Imagine vast armies, each robed in their kingdom's colors, with flagmen waving the crest of their kings. Ranked officers, astride horses and camels, with foot soldiers and artillery face off "in the vale of Siddim" (the Salt Sea). That would make an awesome novel, and the title is built right in: In the Vale of Siddim.

The people served their king for twelve years, rebelled in the thirteenth year, and were smote by the king and his allies in the fourteenth year. In the movie version, this back-story would be dubbed over the intro images by a narrator, letting the audience know the events leading up to the moment our story begins, like they do in *300* and *Lord of the Rings*.

As a writer, it can be tricky to start a book with relevant back story or prologue in most cases. It's easy for the writing to come across "telling" or "teaching" and the audience feels a great distance from the narrative. Plus, the reader has no vested interest yet. There is no main character to cheer for or any established emotional ties because the story hasn't started yet. So how do you deliver back-story without losing the reader? Get characters, relationships, story problems, and setting well-grounded way before the segway into epic battles and many kings.

In my novel *Dreadlands* there is a prophecy book that explains the backstory, but I didn't share the ancient text on page one or in an unnecessary prologue. I didn't even let the main character, Arud, open the book when he first discovered it. I waited until the story was moving along and needed a break to introduce the back-story over several different chapters, not in one sitting. One day, I hope to release this prophecy book as a kindle side story. More to come on that approach in a later chapter.

Author Davis Bunn teaches that your story should open as a door that the reader must run through to catch up. That is rarely if ever accomplished with a prologue or backstory. Movies, of course, are different. *Star Wars* uses the opening scene of each film to display written narrative backstory, and it works. The same is true of *Hunger Games* and *The Teenage Mutant Ninja Turtles* film. The exception? Sequels. Book two can break the backstory rule. Why? Vested interest. The reader is back, which means they care.

Look at your work-in-progress. Have you opened the scene in a moment or a memory? What information can you cut out and paste back into the story in small snippets after the story problem and characters are established? How much of the backstory is for you, the author, to understand the characters and problems? Is it necessary for the reader to know this information?

It's crucial to know what is for you and what is for your reader. That's why I believe most prologues are unnecessary, and when I'm editing a book for a client, I take prologues out almost every time. In fact, 9 times out of 10 you can read, understand, and enjoy the novel without ever needing to know a single detail from a prologue.

So next, let's talk about the folly of the cliché. The guy with his face painted in desert camo, girded with daggers and shields, sneaking into camp in the middle of the night, and slitting his enemy's throats. What if I told you the guy was a bus driver or a soccer dad or a dentist? Now, he's interesting.

It's so easy to fall into the trap: the dumb jock, the blonde bimbo, the shy nerd, and the sweet girl-next-door. Shake things up! Characters that break the mold are far more likely to stick with your reader. Think about Shrek and Monk and Ender Wiggin. These characters are the wrong species, have psychological issues, or are way too young to be playing their roles. But they work brilliantly.

Where have you written lazy cliché characters? How can you adjust or change them to break the mold and create unique, organic characters your reader won't forget? Remember, your story is original, populated by characters with enough backstory to engage the reader while pushing the plot forward.

Have you opened the scene in a moment or a memory? How can you make it a stronger opening?

_____

_____

_____ .

What information can you cut out and paste back into the story in small snippets after the story problem and characters are established?

_____

_____

_____ .

Where have you written lazy cliché characters?

_____

_____

_____ .

How can you adjust or change them to break the mold and create unique, organic characters your reader won't forget?

_____

_____

_____

_____

_____ .

Chapter Ten:

The Sidekick

I'm sure you have a few close friends whose opinions and advice you esteem, who you lean on and trust. Your characters should also. And like in real life, where the people you love can still hurt you, your character's friends, confidants, and mentors shouldn't be static. In fact, sometimes they become antagonists.

The textbook definition of an antagonist is someone or something that prevents or hinders the protagonist from reaching their goal. Could it be the villain? Of course. But could it also be a friend getting in the way? Now you're writing interesting fiction.

In *Goblet of Fire*, Ron becomes a stumbling block for Harry. He behaves as an antagonist for a while, until he finally believes Harry would never have put his name in the goblet on purpose. He changes his tune, believes his BFF, and returns to his role as the sidekick we love.

The love interest can also fluctuate in their role and become a temporary antagonist. They can, like Ron, cross the line between love and hate rather quickly and easily, without anyone holding a grudge.

In *Supernatural*, Cas moves from friend to foe. Initially, he helps Sam and Dean, but by the next season, he fights against them. Because he is a friend first and a foe second, it is hard for us to hate him. We want him to come back to the fold. We hope he will snap out of it and get his crap together. On the other hand, for a true enemy, like Crowley, we know exactly what we're getting into. While for a moment he has a bro-mance with Dean, we don't want him to stick around any longer than he must. Why? We don't trust him.

Using this template, your secondary characters, friends, and sidekicks should be there to pick your protagonist up when he falls, willing to do whatever it takes to help her reach her goal. When they don't, their role can shift to antagonist, if only for a short while.

I think the ultimate sidekick is Samwise Gamgee. Sam is so dedicated to this role that he literally carries Frodo up the slopes of Mount Doom to help him reach his goal. I'm going to compare to Sam throughout this chapter because he really was so well-written and is a character worth modeling your sidekick after.

How is Sam a good friend? Let's try a friend litmus test and see where he falls in the spectrum: A good friend tells the truth at all costs. They don't sugar coat and they don't hold back to spare your feelings. They don't manipulate. They tell it how it is. I see Samwise in all of those, don't you?

Who wants a close friend to tell you what you want to hear, regardless of whether it's in your best interest? Those are the characters in fiction that we expect to backstab or double-cross our main character when the going gets tough. Think Peter Pettigrew from *Harry Potter*, Dennis Nedry from *Jurassic Park*, and Cypher from *The Matrix*.

In my novella *The Dredge*, (spoiler alert) a beautiful girl named Chantelle seduces Marrok to steal his secrets and rise in the ranks of their society. She goes from love interest to backstabbing antagonist with one decision.

As an author, we weave our own message into our books. We sometimes take our experiences and retell them through plot points apparent throughout the entire story. This is how we, as story gods, must approach storytelling with the characters we create.

To write books that don't suck, you must dig down deep and not be afraid to face those relationships from your past that have turned sour. Those love interests who have back stabbed. The friends who turned frenemies. Or the time you were the antagonist in another's story world. Take the emotions and experiences from these relationships and pour them onto the pages of your books to produce fiction that readers will fall in love with. But it takes you facing your demons first to find those characters.

Samwise is often the voice of reason in Frodo's world, speaking the truth when no one else will. He speaks the truth even when Frodo doesn't want to hear it. Likewise, Jiminy Cricket plays conscious to Pinocchio. Timothy Q. Mouse plays the perfect sidekick to Dumbo, as he speaks truth and encouragement, forcing Dumbo to reach for his goals.

The characters influencing your protagonist must serve their purpose well. They need to be supportive, yet truthful. Selfless, yet honest.

Have you created a sidekick who has the courage to speak the truth and the strength to carry the burden when the hero can't? In what ways can you show conflict and tension between them as the protagonist fights against the sidekick's good intentions? What happens when the protagonist refuses to comply?

In the next chapter, we'll look at how even a friend can become an antagonist when they interfere with the protagonist reaching their goals.

Have you created a sidekick who has the courage to speak the truth and the strength to carry the burden when the hero can't?

_____
_____
_____ .

In what ways can you show conflict and tension between them as the protagonist fights against the sidekick's good intentions?

_____
_____
_____ .

What happens when the protagonist refuses to comply?

_____
_____
_____ .

Are you able to create a love interest or friend who ends up betraying the main character? What characteristics must you include. List 3-5.

_____
_____
_____
_____
_____ .

Chapter Eleven:

Friend or Foe?

To continue from the previous chapter, we will now take a deeper look into how a secondary character can become an antagonist by thwarting the protagonist's plans to reach a goal. They don't have to be evil or a nemesis, just a misleading interference.

Let's take a beautiful love interest. We can imply she uses her looks to her advantage when necessary, perhaps as a crafty and cunning woman would. What if she couldn't have children? And what if a prophecy came about that promised her a son? Imagine her impatience getting the better of her and, using her beauty, twisting things around. By convincing her husband that it isn't through her womb from which the prophetic son will be given, but rather through her maidservant, she forces her husband to impregnate someone else. The son is conceived, thereby fulfilling the prophecy by the wife steering the ship.

But there is a fatal flaw here. This is not the hero's journey. His path has been foretold through the prophecy, and he believes it will come to pass as it's written. Through whatever sexual sorcery or logistics, the wife used against him, she convinced her husband to take matters into his own hands.

She becomes an antagonist.

Then, imagine the prophecy comes to pass and the barren wife gives birth. What sort of tension will now exist between the wife, husband, maidservant, and the children? The wife will hate the maidservant and her child who poses a threat to her son. The husband will be stuck between the women and the boys, both of which are his, one of which is his firstborn. The maidservant will be abused by the wife because of the hierarchy in place. Nothing good can come when characters tempt the fates, especially with a prophecy.

Of course, these are great dynamics to push any story along, but this wasn't the hero's journey. It wasn't the plan. This event took the story in a new direction in which it was never meant to go. It brought in a thread that was never intended or written in the outline. The love interest became the villain, and now the hero must choose.

As writers, we can utilize this story function to naturally create tension and strife in our characters. By using a trusted secondary character with good intention to logically persuade the protagonist to head in a direction that isn't on the hero's path, he will be forced to correct himself to get back on track. The secondary character will have to face the consequences of their suggestions, causing tension to grow among the two characters.

Now you've created all kinds of threads with lots of possibilities. Will the two reconcile or is the relationship beyond repair? Can the hero get back on her path? What sacrifices must she make now because of this decision?

A very similar tension exists between Harry and Dudley, consistent in each book. Dudley is an antagonist only because his parents play him against Harry. While Dudley is a nasty child, it is only due to his parent's lack of moral direction and the fact that they, too, abuse Harry that Dudley remains a bugger.

Another story that brilliantly uses the altered hero's path after ignoring the prophecy is the film *Looper*. A man travels back in time to kill a leader, who has destroyed society, when he is a child. In this world, the hero is a hired hitman, supposed to kill the time traveler upon his arrival to the present. The only problem is that the hero is that time traveler from a future story thread, and he has come back to force the hero (his younger self) on a different life path. It's an awesome story, and the man pushes himself into a new life that erases his old one, through time-travel laws.

As you look at the relationships between the characters in your stories, do you see opportunities for secondary characters to behave as antagonists? What problems could that cause for the hero who sidesteps his quest? What new layer of agony does the secondary character face alone? The hero?

Deepening the trauma will give depth and life to all your characters and allow secondary characters to face their own problems, consequences, and decisions independent of the hero. When you can give true motives with genuine cause and affect results to minor characters, as well as the protagonist and antagonist, you will populate your story with well-rounded, believable people that your reader may never forget.

Sometimes, these characters can grow so large that they are given their own hero's quest, such as Riddick from *Pitch Black* or Logan (Wolverine) from the *X-Men* franchise.

Will the two reconcile or is the relationship beyond repair?

_____

_____

_____ .

Can the hero get back on her path? What sacrifices must she make now because of this decision?

_____

_____

_____ .

Do you see opportunities for secondary characters to behave as antagonists?

_____

_____

_____ .

What problems could that cause for the hero who sidesteps his quest?

_____

_____

_____ .

What new layer of agony does the secondary character face alone? The hero?

_____

_____

_____ .

Chapter Twelve:

Names Hold Meaning

Every word in your story should count, and any time you can utilize a word for double meaning, it's like BINGO! Have you ever met someone who didn't "look" like their name? It's weird that someone could not "look" like their name, but it's true, isn't it? Names define us. They categorize us. They put us in order. They classify.

Disney is big on this names-hold-double-meanings thing. Aladdin means "faithful" in Arabic. Simba means "lion" in Swahili. Tiana means "princess" in Greek. Even when you don't know the definition, as a reader, discovering the name's meaning adds a layer to the story. You don't have to know it to enjoy the plot, but by knowing it, you get a deeper understanding of the character and the author. Not to mention, these names are usually unique and memorable.

Aladdin.

Simba.

Tiana.

They are not casual, everyday names, which makes the characters easier to remember and distinguished from other characters in your story.

In my novel *Dreadlands*, I chose each name with purpose, based off Norse and Norwegian roots to express each personality. You don't have to know their meaning to enjoy the book, but after you know what these names mean, a new story layer will draw you further into the book. Our words should always be purposed, deliberate, and provoking. If they aren't, they are taking up space.

In a similar vein, each word in your book should create a picture in the reader's mind. If it doesn't, it is also taking up space. For example, using being verbs can be distracting, since you can't picture am, is, are, was, were, be, being, or been. Can you combine them with a stronger verb?

In edits, it's always worth the effort to remove as many words as possible from your book that cannot be imagined. Do you need some of them? Of course. You can't write a paragraph, let alone a novel without words that don't conjure images in your head. Do many new writers overuse words that don't hold picture value? Yes, and it takes away from the story, distracts from the movie in the minds of their readers.

Here's a few examples:

1. She is walking by with a few things in her hands.

2. In a rush, Suzie swept past, her arms a

cornucopia of pencils, pens, and paper.

How about another?

1. The boy is standing around the playground, waiting for another boy to give up his spot so he can take a turn.

2. Ralph stared, arms crossed, his gaze fixed on Todd who pumped the swing with plump legs, his lips turned in a smirk.

In both circumstances, there are words that you cannot see in your mind, though the second example in each is stronger and easier to imagine. Treat each word as a buck. How much can you save by cutting and combining words to craft a more visually stunning novel?

In *The Lord of the Rings*, Mordor means 'Black Land' in Sindarin and 'Land of Shadows' in Quenya. Those are both different elvish languages, by the way. Tolkien went to the extreme with words (yes, you do hear a tinge of jealousy) by inventing different languages and then creating different sects of these imagined languages. To top it off, he chose to give meaning to words, a truly remarkable and gifted writer.

Sometimes the sounds of names work as well, like Hogwarts being a school for witches and wizards. I mean, hog-warts sounds like an ingredient in a spell, the perfect name! Diagon Alley could very well be *diagonally* while Knockturn Alley is *nocturnally*. Grimmauld Place might be *grim old place*, Remus Lupin (wolf-wolf), and Sirius Black (black dog). Malfoy means "bad faith" and the Mirror of Erised is the same as Mirror of Desire, as if the word "desire" is placed in front of a mirror and reflected backwards. Pretty brilliant writing, Ms. Rowling.

Some character's names reflect the opposite, such as Logan in *X-Men*, which means 'Little Hollow.' I think "Wolverine" is more fitting to his personality! Anakin means warrior, and by his choices, he is all but a warrior. He is a traitor and a name like Darth Vadar makes more sense, meaning "Dark Father."

How can you change the names in your novel to reflect the personality of the character? What about the town or the school or corporation's name? Where can you layer the story with word meaning and definitions?

Editing is the time to do these things, not first draft writing. Once you go back through, find places where a name can be changed to bring more layers to those readers who look deeper, those folks who enjoy the outtakes and behind the scene extras. You'll enjoy the process and get excited when readers discover those Easter eggs you've placed along the way.

How much can you save by cutting and combining words to craft a more visually stunning novel?

_____
_____
_____ .

How can you change the names in your novel to reflect the personality of the character?

_____
_____
_____ .

How can you change the names in your novel to reflect the personality of the character?

_____
_____
_____ .

What about the town or the school or corporation's name?

_____
_____
_____ .

Where can you layer the story with word meaning and definitions?

_____
_____
_____ .

Chapter Thirteen:

Choices Have Consequences

Earlier we discussed making it rain, pouring pain and trouble into your character's world in order to bring out the true hero. We touched on consequences, but I'd like to really dive into it here. Everything in life carries a consequence, just like every yes to one choice is a no to every other possibility.

When crafting your characters, you must remember that they will make choices, some that you don't even see coming. Your job is to make sure that you write in the consequence to that action. Don't let them off the hook. And remember, consequences aren't always bad things, but they do exist, and they do close off every other choice.

That's the key.

When Katniss volunteers for her sister, there

are consequences to that decision. While her purpose is to protect her sister, her very decision puts the entire structure of society into instability and rebellion. Those are not entirely bad consequences, in the sense that they eventually lead to a place where peace is restored, and the games are finally over. However, they eventually are the very consequences that lead to her sister's death. Ironic, isn't it?

When Anakin Skywalker flips to the Dark Side to save Padme, he becomes the very thing that destroys her. The irony that his decision leads to her death changes his life forever. Instead of having faith in the Force, restoring order, and finding a way to live as a family with Padme, Luke, and Leah, he becomes Darth Vadar. His fear forced a future that wasn't his journey. His fear destroyed the life he'd wanted more than anything in the universe.

When a utopian world morphs into a dystopian one, this is good storytelling—the perfect place to hold dark secrets. Consequences from one character's decision can affect the entire story universe. Ender destroys a species and it alters his journey. Instead of finding a way home to his sister, he leaves his universe with an understanding that he will never see her again. Instead of destroying the Formics once and for all, he is on a mission to find them a new home for their queen to repopulate her species.

Consequences control character.

Apply this to your world building and plot. Create a world that appears wonderful on the surface, yet harbors something sinister or dangerous beneath.

Invasion of the Body Snatchers.

The Time Machine.

The Lottery by Shirley Jackson.

By giving away small bits of information, you can create a bread trail of curiosity that your reader can't help but follow, page after page.

Thomas Brown's debut novel *Lynnwood* does an excellent job of weaving the sinister through a sleepy town with the hint that something's not right. The *House on Haunted Hill,* also by Shirley Jackson, exemplifies how consequences create plots, even when the strings of time are altered. In the same sense, so does *Stranger Things*, a story teeming in consequence, many of which that leads to the death of beloved characters.

Stephen King and Edgar Allen Poe are the masters of suspense-horror. They both show relatively normal people in relatively normal places, overtaken by either an outside force or, more frequently, by their own dark heart's choices. They show the "what if's" when a person receives exactly what they *think* they want or need.

Thinner.

The Tell-Tale Heart.

The Monkey's Paw, by W.W. Jacobs.

Have you ever made a mistake? Have you ever lost everything because of it? Have you ever had to return to someone you truly wronged to ask for forgiveness? Those are hard consequences to face, but they make terrific plot points.

Position your characters to make choices that lead them to fatal mistakes, which cost them everything, then force them to repent to those they've wronged. You've got a base for great tension and an opportunity to show the dark-heart choices of humanity that your readers can relate to. We don't like to admit it, but we would all agree that selfishness lurks in us all. In our stories, as the clock ticks and time runs out, this evil pushes to the surface, and we see what our characters are truly made of.

In your story, have you allowed your characters to make decisions that appear good, but carry weighty consequences? How can you expand those to ripple out even further in their lives? Into the lives of those around them?

By allowing your characters to give into their own dark-heart desires, you can create a natural set of consequences that will shake their world and bring it crashing to the ground. Then, with the now humbled character, you can help rebuild their life and their world into something great, like Ebenezer Scrooge from Dicken's *A Christmas Carol* or Katniss Everdeen from the *Hunger Games*.

Can you position your characters to make fatal mistakes that cost them everything? How?

_____

_____

_____ .

Will they repent for their wrongdoing or fall victim to their consequence? Explain.

_____

_____

_____ .

Have you allowed your characters to make decisions that appear good, but carry weighty consequences?

_____

_____

_____ .

How can you expand those to ripple out even further in their lives? Into the lives of those around them?

_____

_____

_____ .

Chapter Fourteen:

Real Life Ain't Fair

Real life ain't fair.

Your story reflects real life. Even if it's a fantasy or science fiction, the reader should believe the characters are real, their lives are real, and their situations are real.

So, why is everything working out so easily for them when real life ain't fair?

Overall, life is a system of canyons and mountains. The highs are high, and the lows are low. Much happens between those dips and trips, but often, many of these situations are not fair.

The singer who has an uncle in the industry. Not fair.

The perfect mother and wife who dies young of cancer, when she eats healthy and works out. Not fair.

The other guy/gal who always gets the girl/guy, even when you're the one she/he confides in. Not fair.

So, if life ain't fair, how come your main character knows the precise piece of information required to solve that unsolvable puzzle, no questions asked? Why is it that every plan is perfectly executed with everything she needs in her grasp? That's not real life. Cause real life ain't fair.

I'll tell you a story. My grandmother wanted a great-granddaughter her whole life. I had two kids, two boys, and my brother had none. Then, he and his wife got pregnant, when they turned 40! My grandmother couldn't have been happier, and even told my brother his pregnancy and knowing it was a girl, was the final piece in her life's perfection. What a beautiful moment.

Then, she got sick. Needed a pacemaker. Dr. punctured her lung. Organs shut down. And she died. Less than thirty days before her great-granddaughter was born. Thirty days! A standard procedure that should have brought twenty more years to her life ended it.

Why did this happen?

Cause real life ain't fair.

It wasn't like a movie, where she held the baby in her arms and took her last breath.

Real life ain't fair.

If your fiction mirrors real life, make it hurt, make it pinch, make your reader feel something that makes them uncomfortable. Then, using your god powers, write everything neatly into a beautiful ending they didn't see coming, and they will love you for it. Place that baby in her great-grandmother's arms during her dying breath, because after you show that life ain't fair, you get to make everything right.

When Rue dies in the *Hunger Games*, my inner self screams, "That's not fair!" Yet I knew she was dead from the moment she was introduced in the story. Stories are so powerful because they consider the fact that real life ain't fair and bad things happen to people with good intentions.

What's the point?

Real life ain't fair, and our choices have consequences that ripple and grow and take on lives of their own, sometimes even after we try doing the right thing.

Take Obi Wan Kenobi and Anakin Skywalker. Obi Wan is desperate to teach Anakin the way of the Jedi, knowing he will restore order to the Force. But in the end, Anakin joins Lord Sidious on the Dark Side. Obi Wan did everything right, yet it wasn't enough. Broken-hearted, he loses not just his padawan, but a friend he found to be more like a brother. Why? Say it with me: real life ain't fair. So, your story shouldn't be fair either.

In what areas of your manuscript can you adjust the balance and create more realism? How can you make it harder for your characters to succeed? Where can you bring in the powerlessness from your characters' doing what's right, yet still failing? In what way can you make your story world reflect the real world?

Want a good study example? Read the entire *Maze Runner* series. Talk about unfair!

Real life ain't fair, so let's shake things up in our story's reality. And the best part, as I've already mentioned, is that once you tear your hero's down, you get to build them up because as the story god, you get to bring balance to every unfair act in your story. You get to fix what you broke. You get to undermine the laws of life and nature to leave the world a better place then it started through the eyes of your reader.

In what areas of your manuscript can you adjust the balance and create more realism?

_____
_____
_____ .

How can you make it harder for your characters to succeed?

_____
_____
_____ .

Where can you bring in the powerlessness from your characters' doing what's right, yet still failing?

_____
_____
_____ .

In what way can you make your story world reflect the real world?

_____
_____
_____ .

Chapter Fifteen:

The Prophecy Fulfilled

Many stories center around the prophecy, in which unexplainable and unbelievable circumstances produce a savior, no matter how awkward or un-heroic he or she appears.

Harry Potter.

Luke Skywalker.

Gregor the Overlander.

Percy Jackson.

Clark Kent.

Look at Peter Parker. Uncle Ben says, "With great power comes great responsibility." But Peter doesn't want the gift. He wants a normal life with Mary Jane, one that is not possible for Spiderman. Or Harry Potter, who has spent his entire life in the dark with regards to the world of magic, is suddenly thrust into an environment where he is expected to be the greatest wizard of all time.

The most incredible part of the prophecy

fulfilled story is the hero's journey. Her growth as she doubts herself, denies her gifts, refuses her task, and ignores the needs of the people that only she can fulfill, is something we can all relate to. The hero fails before they become heroic. Even more so, the prophesied one is in a position they never asked for. Can we relate or what?

Ever had a job you hated, a teacher you despised, or a situation you were forced to endure? We all have, and we all will again. Are we the prophesied one? No, of course not. But we can relate to feeling like our voice goes unheard, loss of control of their future, and a desire to rebel against what they were created to be.

It's an awesome and powerful experience that brings the reader alongside the hero to feel her own self-doubt and inabilities and fears as she, too, discovers inner strength, perseverance, and sacrifice for the prophecy's fulfillment.

When you are writing any story, but especially one that centers around the "savior" who comes and disrupts their world, it is important to know before you start if the savior will win, fail, or draw in the end.

Anakin Skywalker set out to become the one to bring balance to the Force. Anakin failed.

His son Luke, on the other hand had the same calling and he succeeded. Luke won.

Katniss Everdeen ends her story (at least book one) as a draw. She wins the games, but does she really win? Her life is now on Snow's radar, and that means her family and those she loves', too. This is a draw, and it takes a few books to get to her win, but even in that sense, did she really win? Losing Prim, the only thing that motivated her to do anything, is a loss that can't be undone. I'd say the overarching story arch is draw for this entire series.

Whether or not you're writing a story with a prophecy, take some time to study books or movies that are based around this element. What emotions were stirred up in you? How did the author accomplish this? Can you diagram the hero's ups and downs? What inner and outer forces contributed to their growth and fallbacks?

As a prophecy is fulfilled and a hero is born, so the same exact environment and circumstances work to create a nemesis, an idea which will be explored in the next chapter.

What emotions are stirred up in you as you follow the life of the unlikely "savior"?

_____

_____

_____ .

How did the author accomplish this?

_____

_____

_____ .

Can you diagram the hero's ups and downs?

_____

_____

_____ .

What inner and outer forces contributed to their growth and fallbacks?

_____

_____

_____ .

At "the end" will your hero/savior fin a win-lose-or-draw?

_____

_____

_____ .

Chapter Sixteen:

The Nemesis

Have you ever thought someone was talking about you when they weren't? Or misinterpreted what they said or their motives? We all have. It happens more often than you'd think, since we interpret most of life through body language, which is why services like social media posts and texts become so toxic so fast.

Notice how rudely people cut you off in their cars. Then, you look in when they pass, and see the profile of a perfectly normal looking human. It's the same thing. We are inside our cone of shame and therefore, have no body language to speak through. Unless you count the middle finger. Touché.

According to Dr. Albert Mehrabian, 93% of all communication is non-verbal communication. (www.nonverbalgroup.com) That means 7% of communication comes from actual dialogue. Your characters should be filled with gestures, facial expressions, sarcasm, vocal tones, posture, etc., even more so than quipped dialogue.

Do your characters convey exactly what they always feel? Do they lie, stretch the truth, soften the blow, or constrict around certain characters and relax around others? These are physiological responses, whether on purpose or reactionary, that must be in your books if you want your characters to move from two-dimensional to three-dimensional.

The Emotion Thesaurus by Angela Ackerman and Becca Puglisis is an excellent resource of mental and physical responses to emotions. Plus, they have developed this series into many books that focus on villains, heroes, and more. Put them on your wish list.

A great, often used plot line, is the evil stepmother who abuses or resents her stepchildren. They are connected by the natural parent, someone whom they both love. *Cinderella* is the most obvious example, but variations of this plot can be seen even in the relationship between Harry Potter and the Dursleys or between the siblings in *The Man in the Iron Mask*.

The best hero also has a piece of the villain inside him. While *Harry Potter* took that literally with the lightning bolt horcrux, other stories have been more subtle. Take the relationship with Professor X and Magneto. At one time, Charles Xavier and Eric Lehnsherr were besties. They discovered their gifts and fought the world together, arguing and doing life side by side. While they went separate ways, it wasn't because they were enemies. Rather it was because they had a very different opinion on their core beliefs: the future of Mutants. Giving them such a deep, connection and history, made their friendship and consequential falling out more powerful.

When I watched the first *X-Men* movie, where Professor X and Magneto are old men, I looked at them as the good guy and the bad guy. When I saw the films when they were young men, my heart flipped. I learned to love Eric and respect Charles' decision. They each held a piece of the other inside them, and so did I.

When the nemesis is the hero, who has made different life choices based off self-serving interests instead of the selflessness of the world, it makes for a splendid relationship. It forces the reader to love and hate them both simultaneously.

On the flipside, when you have a character like Dumbledore, painted as the selfless guide, at odds with someone like Snape, painted as the self-serving sniveler, and you are able, at the last minute, to flip the reader's view, you've crafted magic. Rowling causes my heart to ache alongside Snape and feel hatred with understanding toward Dumbledore. It was the only way. I know this, and it makes the nemesis and hero relationship vibrant.

Having deep, common bonds between the hero and the nemesis make their conflict stronger. Using an outside force or character to force the separation pushes the problem to grow and the emotions to deepen between the hero and the villain.

Superman and Zod.

Harry Potter and Voldemort.

Thomas and WICKED.

These relationships both attract and repel simultaneously because of the bonds between and similarities of the two opposing characters. It highlights their differences and shapes them into those figures we can't forget, long after we've read "The End."

Do your characters convey exactly what they always feel?

_____
_____
_____ .

What ticks in physical behavior can you use to show this fact of body language verses spoken word?

_____
_____
_____ .

Have you created a well-rounded nemesis who shares a past with the hero?

_____
_____
_____ .

In what ways can you deepen the relationship or the past between your hero and your villain?

_____
_____
_____ .

Chapter Seventeen:

Parallels

Finding ways to parallel events in your story is not difficult. Sometimes, you plan it and do it on purpose. Other times, you discover through edits that you are a better writer than you realized. You've set up similarities throughout your work that jump out during edits or through the keen eye of good beta readers.

When you see minor parallels you've built into your narrative, your job is to take what you planted and grow it. Highlight those story threads by bringing them into focus later in the story. The trick is to leave breadcrumb sized mortals, not entire loafs. You don't want the strings to be too obvious, yet you also want them to be clear enough that the reader notices.

It can be subtle, like Frodo becoming more and more like Gollum under the ring's power or it can be the pivotal point in the story, like Harry Potter and Voldemort's connection, even unto death. In the story, both Voldemort and Harry share a phoenix core in their wands, both are orphans, and both face death. One fears it so much he separates his soul to avoid it, while the other faces it so often, he willingly enters it.

In *Hunger Games*, Katniss parallels to the Mockingjay and becomes a physical embodiment of the symbolism. This is a great way to establish a parallel, through an item, a piece of jewelry, a wand (and it doesn't hurt for merchandising after the book is published.)

In my story *Exposure*, there's a tattoo that appears on the kids' necks, one I will get the day the book goes under contract. It will also translate to temporary tattoos as giveaways and stickers. Consider adding in parallels that can translate later to products to enhance your readers' experience.

Parallels are also fun for the reader. When they discover something of interest and then see it bloom into a major plot point later in the story, they feel clever and a part of your world. We do it naturally, try to connect dots and string things together, to make sense of our world. We look for those moments in films and books, too. And then, when it happens, we say, "I knew it!" You want to set up those moments for your reader. They will love you for it!

Another way to parallel is throughout a series. If you think about the lives of Anakin and Luke, they are parallels of one another throughout a multiple film series. *The Back to the Future* trilogy is riddled with parallels, and after watching it about eighty-eighty times (see what I did there?), I still find Easter eggs and parallels every time.

Ready Player One is another incredible book filled with parallels and Easter eggs. It literally shows people from the real world and the parallel image of themselves in the game, the Oasis. The whole book focuses on finding the parallels in the game from the life of the game's creator, in order to win the ultimate prize, left in his will and shared through his digital avatar. It's an incredible book if you've not read it yet, and a killer film worth watching a million times at least.

Where have you established parallels in your story that could be drawn bolder? Are your protagonist and antagonist on similar paths? How can you show one decide toward destruction while the other, faced with the same circumstances, chooses life?

Building in these "aha" moments will build a following of readers who can't wait for you to release your next book, which is, after all, what most authors are hoping for.

Where have you established parallels in your story that could be drawn bolder?

_____
_____
_____ .

How are your protagonist and antagonist on similar paths?

_____
_____
_____ .

How can you show one decide toward destruction while the other, faced with the same circumstances, chooses life?

_____
_____
_____ .

Have you set up parallels in book one that you can draw out in book two? Name 3-5, even if you never write the second book in the series.

_____
_____
_____ .

Chapter Eighteen:

Rules

We all have rules in our lives. Rituals, customs, laws, and the lore that surround them govern our decisions and our families, our instincts, even our dreams. No greater element of realism can bring depth and dimension to your story than the rules. And I'm not just talking science fiction or fantasy.

So how important are rituals, customs, laws, and lore in stories? Strong convictions of belief and ritual create entire storylines. They provide the world in which our characters will follow or fight. The Civil Wars in the *Hunger Games* led to the formation of Panem under the Capital, and the distinctions of the districts. The establishment of the games set into action a constant reminder of the peace the Capital brought to the districts.

The Jedi are the religious sect of the *Star Wars* universe. They wear robes, wield magic, and follow clear cut laws, such as no marriage and no politics.

Their customs are foundational in this world, and without them, Anakin's struggle would have no base. He loves Padme and wants to start a family with her. But her political position and his life as a Jedi prevent their affair from happening in their society. The laws of their culture run deep. In fact, dozens of books have been written on the lore alone, debated in chat rooms and at comic conventions around the globe.

The Formic Wars that caused the near extinction of Earth led to the recruitment and training of children to battle an alien species under the guise of a game. This is the world of Ender Wiggin. In a way, it's like Katniss's world, a place where laws dictate the treatment of children and the jobs they possess in the future... whether they like it or not.

The rules of *Twilight* were slightly different than those of traditional vampire lore, giving the story world a fresh approach to a classic monster. These beautiful beings had sparkling skin (that was amazing in the book, and a good laugh in the film rendition), and they were able to walk in sunlight, which I thought was a cool twist. It worked because Meyer's changed the rules, established those rules, and gave history behind them so they made sense. It wasn't happenstance, it was purposed.

Your rules must be established in the story before you begin to populate it with characters.

When I wrote *Dreadlands*, I filled the world with story lore and rules. My first draft editing process was to go page by page and find every mention of the lore. Then, I looked at only that portion of the story to confirm that my lore made sense, didn't contradict itself, and worked.

How important is this, you ask?

The lore and world building and laws of Harry Potter were so impactful to readers that it was built in real life. You can go to Universal Studios and walk the streets of Diagon Alley, buy a wand at Olivander's, or see a version of Hogwarts in Islands of Adventure. And believe me, the rules of Hogwarts apply. The wands show magic in the real world, although through digital means, that make you feel like you have stepped into Rowling's universe.

What customs and laws have you created for your story world? How deep does the lore run? Have you constructed a unique lore with rules that force the characters to comply or rebel? Can you take current lore and tweak it to be your own?

Constructing a deep-rooted story world with rituals, customs, laws, and lore will keep your story from toppling over. As with a tree, where the larger the trunk and boughs, the greater the root system must be for balance, your story needs lore that runs deep to balance what is taking place on the page. And you don't need to write it all in one book. You can save it for companion novellas or short stories to share with your truest fans.

What customs and laws have you created for your story world?

_____
_____
_____ .

How deep does your lore run and where can you strengthen it?

_____
_____
_____ .

Have you constructed a unique lore with rules that force the characters to comply or rebel?

_____
_____
_____ .

Can you take current lore, like vampires or werewolves, and tweak it to be your own?

_____
_____
_____ .

Chapter Nineteen:

Plotting Coincidence

Sometimes, truth is stranger than fiction. I hear stories or watch events unfold and say to myself, "If I wrote that in a book, no one would believe it." Yet life is filled with bizarre coincidence, strange similarities, and predetermined paths.

How can we learn to build believable predictions within our story worlds? How can we mimic life's invariable ebb and flow by plotting coincidence?

I wrote a short story once about a girl who auctioned her virginity to pay for school. Bizarre, you say? It was from an article I read in the newspaper. Want more? A gaming company eliminated the Twin Towers from their programming due to space constraints, stating that the buildings were attacked by terrorists. This occurred a year before the bombing. James Dean died in a car crash weeks after endorsing a drive safe campaign for the National Safety Council.

A 1990s episode of Quantum Leap shows Sam watching Super Bowl XXX, where the Steelers are down by three. Guess who was in Super Bowl XXX and ended the game down by three? And who could forget the seventeenth episode of season eleven of the Simpsons, where Donald Trump is the US President? Don't tell me that coincidences don't happen in real life.

How do we craft coincidence?

By definition, a coincidence is a, well... coincidence, "a remarkable concurrence of events or circumstances without apparent casual connection." (Oxford) How do you write a connection that is supposed to look unconnected and casually connected at the same time? It is not easy to do.

I recommend you have your characters ask themselves probing questions. Then, let the narrative show them finding those answers. After you have written the entire novel, go back and add casual coincidence to connect these plot points in a subtle way. Next, add inner thoughts, where the characters notice similarities, or signs, that they connect to their own plot.

These moments connect the reader to your characters. They allow the reader to draw upon their own emotions through empathy or sympathy to care about your characters. And if done correctly, both your characters and your readers will believe in the coincidence, one that you wrote on purpose, which makes you a genius, by the way.

When Harry Potter needed to learn more about Nicholas Flammel and lacked a way into the restricted area of the library, did the appearance of the invisibility cloak feel like a far-fetched coincidence? Or perfect timing? It felt like perfect timing because this sort of thing had been happening to Harry all along, from the letters at the Dursleys to the introduction to Hagrid. We believed that someone was watching Harry, so we didn't feel it was contrived when the cloak appeared. It brought up more questions for us to bond with Harry, as we both wondered where it came from and who sent it. That's good writing.

When Katniss was stuck in a tree with tributes sleeping at the base, was it a contrived addition to have not only Rue appear, but for her to show Katniss the tracker jacker hive that just so happened to be hanging off the branch right above her? Or was it the handiwork of a crafty author who expertly manifested coincidence out of thin air? Tracker Jacker nests were all over the arena. Why wouldn't one be hanging near where Katniss slept? We believe it because the solution was presented before the need arose.

That's the trick to bringing believable coincidence into a story: state or show it before you need it, not after.

If we had never seen Katniss shoot an arrow or hunt or forage or trap, it would be an awfully unbelievable coincidence to suddenly see her exhibit these behaviors in the Games. And if we never saw Ender as an expert problem solver and true leader, it would be hard to swallow when he outwits the adults and ends their war. And Harry, well, if no one had helped him before, we would wonder, "why now?" and it would suck us out of the story and into disbelief.

Your reader is smart. They want to find the threads and connect them before the characters, but they don't want to be fed solutions that don't make sense. They want to believe there is order beneath the disorder, but they don't want to feel like the coincidence has been manufactured. Your writing needs to be concise, clever, and crafty to both please the reader and challenge the characters.

Have you shown your characters solving their problems with convenient coincidences or have you taken the time to plot them into believable situations? Where have you written in set-ups, but never followed through with delivery? This can frustrate your reader who spends the time waiting for you to follow through on a promise you made to them in the set-up you've written. Make sure you don't forget to close out the set-up with a solution.

Coincidences happen every day and people naturally connect the dots to arrive at end results to force order into their lives. By building in set-ups with solutions, you will add layers of believability to your characters and story world by leading to coincidences that don't just make sense, they make fact of your fiction.

How can we learn to build believable predictions within our story worlds?

_____
_____
_____ .

How can we mimic life's invariable ebb and flow by plotting coincidence?

_____
_____
_____ .

Have you shown your characters solving their problems with convenient coincidences or have you taken the time to plot them into believable situations?

_____
_____
_____ .

Where have you written in set-ups, but never followed through with delivery?

_____
_____
_____ .

Chapter Twenty:

Play-Rewind-Repeat

Who doesn't love a story with some good sibling rivalry?

Supernatural is my all-time favorite series, and when they aren't fighting demons, angels, and every monster in between, Sam and Dean are usually fighting each other. They have competition issues. Sam feels like he made the wrong choices and should have stayed in law school. Dean feels like he needs to protect Sam at all costs. They both have different perspectives and memories of their father and they both feel personally responsible for the death of their mother. They hide secrets, relationships, and misdeeds from one another on a regular basis. It's a man soap opera, and we absolutely love it.

Cinderella is the unwanted threat to her new step-sisters. She is beautiful, even though her new family does its best to keep her covered in soot and dirt, doing all the chores. Beauty comes from the inside out, and the ugly step-sisters see it shining through. "Pleasing mother" is the shared goal of all the sisters, though Cinderella's disadvantage makes it impossible. The step-mother sees her dead husband in Cinderella's eyes, remembers his kindness through Cinderella's obedience, and hears his voice through phrases Cinderella repeats.

Many times, we inherit our family's flaws. We swear we never will _____ and end up doing _____, as adults. At some point in the game, against our best will power, we become our parents. Shouldn't our characters do the same? The good ones do, and many of them continue the story where mommy or daddy left off.

Play-Rewind-Repeat.

Sam and Dean don't want to be hunters. They hunt because it was passed down to them by their father.

Play-Rewind-Repeat.

President Coin tried to continue the games as punishment to the Capital, using the Capital's children as tribute. Of course, Katniss had other ideas.

Play-Rewind-Repeat.

I think these relational setups cannot be ignored. They are universal and powerful and dark and deep. They are the side of good that rises to the surface when life is heated up. They reveal character. Unchecked, these sins are passed down to the next generation. They are a warning of what our lives can become if we are not careful and aware of the generational consequences of our choices.

As writers, it is our privilege to mimic the world around us, but with the power to make things right again, to bring balance to the Universe by "the end" as we restore order in a chaotic life. Characters who act because of generational predetermination or genetic cursing is extremely powerful. It's the lifeline behind *A Christmas Carol*, the greatest fear in Ender Wiggin's heart, and the essence of Harry Potter's quest to not just defeat but understand Voldemort. Folly repeating folly is real life, but folly overcoming folly is the magic of storytelling.

Let's start by finding places where our characters are faced with identical choices to those in their past or in the past of someone they are close to. How can you show tension in this moment? Will he take the familiar, easy path or the unknown road toward redemption and rebirth? Have you shown her inner struggle as she tries not to become what she fears she is destined to be? What about those fears about becoming who the world expects her to be although she feels unequipped for the challenge?

In life, we often find that we repeat the same mistakes several times before we get it right. Maybe it's a family curse, like in *Holes*, that has been put on our shoulders to make right. More likely it's the younger version of ourselves swearing we will never grow up and become like this person or that person, only to find out we have. It isn't easy to overcome these flaws, these curses, and many of us are never able to achieve that success. But in our books, where we are guaranteed the ability to restore order, these flaws and innate hurdles are the traits our budding heroes need to grow into the saviors of our stories.

How can you show tension in those moments when your characters face identical choices to those in their past or in the past of someone they are close to?

_____
_____
_____ .

Have you shown her inner struggle as she tries not to become what she fears she is destined to be?

_____
_____
_____ .

What about those fears about becoming who the world expects her to be although she feels unequipped for the challenge?

_____
_____
_____ .

Have you built in a family curse that can be driven home through additional backstory? How can you deliver this best to your reader?

_____
_____
_____ .

Chapter Twenty-One:

Trust Through Blind Faith

Trust is a tricky concept. It's something we are expected to give, reluctant to release, and impossible to regain once broken. Blind faith, on the other hand, recalls two of my top ten favorite characters in literature: Frodo Baggins and Harry Potter.

Frodo and Harry are both given plights that are much more intense than originally let on to be. They are both tasked with saving their worlds and they both lose themselves in the process. In each circumstance, these unlikely heroes were only given a partial truth on which they based acceptance of the quest. Naively, through blind faith, they entered into their unwritten contracts to do something simple, like carry a ring to a mountain or go to a school for wizards.

Both are thrust into situations that are much greater than they had originally been told or thought. Both are constantly reminded of the great task that has been burdened to them. Both are betrayed by those they were expected to depend upon. Both place trust through blind faith on the world and direction given to them by a great father figure with substantial supernatural powers.

Crafting blind trust can be tricky. You don't want your main character to come across as weak, dumb, or careless. Once again, you are expected to purposefully create something that comes across as casual. It's not an easy task. Your hero needs to grow and that means they must start small. Like you, your characters should, given the chance, make different decisions in their past based off the life lessons they've acquired throughout the story.

If you were eighteen again, knowing what you know now, would you make the same decisions? Would you have blind faith in the same people? Would you enter relationships as casually as your younger self? Doubtful. What about you in your twenties? Thirties? You get my point. Your character should be no different.

If Frodo knew what he knew in the end of *The Lord of the Rings* trilogy in the beginning, would he have made the journey? Maybe, maybe not. That's not the point, is it? The point is that your character will begin, like you did, filled with trust through blind faith. Then, when life hits with disappointment and false hope, they will change, chiseled and formed into the hero they were destined to become.

Can you find places in your writing where your character's trust through blind faith led to places that make it seem like they've made the wrong decision? How can you increase the tension through the betrayal of others? Did you include a steadfast character to remind the hero of his journey and to encourage him to stay on the path? Are there highly respected authority figures who are larger than life guarding the character along their quest?

It's a very scary and unguarded feeling to trust with blind faith, but it gives depth to your characters. It really gives the reader a vested emotional interest in the outcome. When it seems unfair, we get angry and demand justice. And when justice comes by "the end" in whatever form the writer sees fit, we feel satisfied as a reader that order has been restored to the universe once again. If only for a short while.

Can you find places in your own writing where your characters trust through blind faith only to be led into places that make it seem like they've made the wrong decision?

_____

_____

_____ .

How can you increase the tension through the betrayal of others?

_____

_____

_____ .

Did you include a steadfast character to remind the hero of his journey and to encourage him to stay on the path?

_____

_____

_____ .

Are there highly respected authority figures who are larger than life guarding the character along their quest?

_____

_____

_____ .

Chapter Twenty-Two:

Trickery & Betrayal

Betrayal is a powerful tool, and what better topic to follow one on *Trust & Blind Faith* then *Trickery & Betrayal*. Often, blind faith results in betrayal.

In *Hunger Games*, Katniss naively trusts Peeta, since technically, they became enemies the second their names were called. The trickery begins when Peeta asks to train alone, and the betrayal occurs when he joins forces with the District 1 and 2 pack to hunt her down. We know his intentions are pure, that he is using trickery against Tributes to protect Katniss, but she doesn't. The betrayal is painful, when she climbs the tree and looks down upon him, that boy from her district, who tells the others to wait her out and kill her when she comes down to eat.

Harsh!

In *Maze Runner*, the trickery and betrayal run so deep, you don't know what is really happening until the final line in the last book of the series. Everyone's motives are questionable. It's a great cat and mouse story because at some point everyone is the cat, and everyone is the mouse. But the major betrayal is from Teresa, when she calls WICKED and releases the location of the base that has welcomed them in with open arms.

Ouch!

Betrayal in life can be a deal breaker, one of those things you may never recover from. And when it's performed through trickery, the wound can stay opened forever.

Build these actions into your novels. Let your heroes and villains alike be betrayed by their closest confidantes. Good writing happens when you can craft these scenes and are still able to show both parties are correct in one way or another.

For example, most of the time, people blame shift, finger point, and excuse their own behavior rather than fess up. They believe themselves, fall into their own story so deeply, that they might even forget that there is another side to the story. Perspective is a powerful tool, and you should use it to show the motives of betrayal.

In *Harry Potter*, Ron totally bails on Harry in *The Goblet of Fire*, believing that Harry put his name in on purpose. Later in the books, he accuses Harry of being jealous because he is finally getting attention over Harry, when Ron gets the position as Keeper and the girl (as crazy as she might be). We are angry with his betrayal, but we also understand it because Rowling is a brilliant writer. Ron is the muddle in the middle, the child without notice, who is always trying to find fame. Harry couldn't care less about fame but can't seem to escape it. We are mad at Ron for being a jerk, but we get it.

Plus, we can relate.

We've been that friend. We've had that friend. This type of betrayal is easier to forgive and forget, unlike the Teresa-bomb discussed earlier. That one is a deal breaker. Think about human shortcomings as you create round, believable characters.

What ways can you deliver believable trickery and betrayal into your stories? Subtlety works well. Keeping the reader in the dark alongside the protagonist is great, like Katniss in *Catching Fire* and Harry Potter at the end of the series with Snape and Dumbledore. It's also effective to show the truth in treachery to the reader, who will helplessly watch broken-hearted as the betrayal is revealed, like Obi-Won with Anakin Skywalker in *Revenge of the Sith* or the old hag who's really the wicked queen in *Snow White.*

Remember to always show the price the character must pay in exchange for their betrayal. If there is no cost, there is no stake. If there's nothing at stake, your reader won't care.

In your story, where have you let people off the hook too easily? Have you set up moments of trickery and betrayal? Did the audience know in advance or was it revealed to them at the same time as the character? Why? How much does the reveal affect the emotional impact to both main character and reader?

Trickery and betrayal happen in everyday life, from tiny decisions that may go unnoticed (revealing the true heart of your character and foreshadowing a greater deceit to come) to major events that alter lives, relationships, and even the future of the universe in one way or another. The degree to which you incorporate the treachery into your story will make it more believable and the resulting anger, hatred, and even vengeance to kill in exchange for the deceit will bring depth and heartache to an otherwise perfect story world.

Where have you let characters off the hook too easily?

_____

_____

_____ .

Have you set up moments of trickery and betrayal?

_____

_____

_____ .

Did the audience know in advance or was it revealed to them at the same time as the main character? Why?

_____

_____

_____ .

How much does the reveal affect the emotional impact to both main character and reader?

_____

_____

_____ .

Chapter Twenty-Three:

Showing Inner Struggles

There are basically two types of people in the world and they are labeled as glass half-full or half-empty. Some people go through life seeing all its potential, taking the bull by the horns, and making lemonade from lemons. Others flounder from feeling to feeling, seeing life as the result of events strung together, riding a rollercoaster of ups and downs, as they take life's lemons and suck on them until their teeth hurt.

We all have problems. Everyone from the richest to the poorest, from the healthiest to the sickest, to the young and old alike. The issue isn't the *have* it's the *how*.

How do you handle life when it isn't fair?

How do you handle people when they aren't fair?

How do you handle *you* when things don't go your way?

Now ask these same questions of your

characters and you're ready to write fiction.

To create characters that emulate real life, you must study real life. When writing, your characters must display human emotions of confusion, self-doubt, shame, and heartache. Or aloofness, bitterness, envy, and malice. These dynamics make great characters. We can feel their emotions as we imagine ourselves in their shoes or remember a time when we were in their place. And a great way to accomplish this is by making things not what they appear to be.

Eleven from *Stranger Things* is a great example of living in an emotional roller coaster. She is distraught throughout the entire series, desperate to avoid her father, haunted to find her mother, and curious about the new sister she discovers downtown. She is called to become something that she never asked to become. Her powers are generated and in turn, they generate a world that she is responsible for, even though it brings forth nothing but destruction.

She is kept from her friends, lied to, and tasked with saving the world, while dealing with all the teenage angst puberty brings. Think of the pressure, guilt, anger, frustration, love, and hope that flow through her at all times? She is an incredible character because she is emotional.

Have you created characters the reader can empathize with regardless of their right or wrong status, like Severus Snape and Anakin Skywalker? Will the reader feel the inner struggle as your main character fights and-or accepts their destiny whether they believe it or not, like Ender Wiggin or Katniss Everdeen? Did you remember to bring in a character to affirm the main character's role, like Glenda to Dorothy or Timothy E. Mouse to Dumbo?

One of the most difficult parts of inner turmoil is showing it to the reader. It's inside the main character, so the tendency is to tell the reader what they are feeling. That is the best way to write a book that sucks, and since you are trying to write a book that doesn't suck, let's consider ways of showing instead. Find unique ways to share these inner struggles.

Technology is a way to have characters interact, whether they post on social in your story or exchange a series of texts/snaps with a friend. How about a journal? Your hero could journal every third chapter at the start of the chapter. I've seen famous quotes beneath the chapter header in some books. Maybe you could find famous quotes that mirror the hero's inner struggle for each chapter and use that to get inside of their heads and hearts without "telling" the reader what they are feeling. They could see a shrink, confide in an animal, meditate, have lucid dreams, hear voices... the story world is your oyster.

Take some time to have your characters share their inner turmoil, fears, and life questions. Show their insecurities and flaws in their decisions, dialogue, and choices.

Han Solo sticks in our minds because he redeems himself by returning to fight. In the whole story, he is set up as self-absorbed, untrustworthy, and emotionally-driven. But in the end, he makes the right choice and we love him for it.

Name 3-5 characters you've created that your reader can empathize with regardless of their behavior. Include specific instances.

_____
_____
_____
_____
_____ .

Share specific details of why the reader will feel the inner struggle as your main character fights and-or accepts their destiny.

_____
_____
_____ .

Have you crafted a guide to bring your hero affirmation of their quest and role? Describe them.

_____
_____
_____ .

How do your main characters handle life when it isn't fair? Handle others who behave unfairly? React when things don't go their way?

_____
_____
_____
_____
_____ .

Chapter Twenty-Four:

The Love Triangle

Ah, the power of love.

Romeo and Juliet.

Edward and Bella.

Shrek and Fiona.

But what happens when that third person enters the scene? When Jacob vies for Bella's heart, when Katniss feels torn between Peeta and Gale, or when Prince Charming locks Shrek up and steals his identity? Plot happens, that's what.

The characteristics that make a love triangle work are someone wants love, but can't attain it, and someone else attains love, but doesn't find happiness.

If Katniss loved Gale and found happiness with him, she never would have had eyes for Peeta outside of the arena. But even during the games, we saw that spark of attraction between them. Maybe not love, but it was enough to keep us watching. And, like I said, if Katniss was happy with Gale, this never would have happened.

Other times, human nature comes into play, breaking up a perfectly lovely relationship through betrayal, lies, envy, jealousy, and deception. There's a fine line between love and hate because most people who hate someone they once loved still love them. When you stop loving someone, you don't care what they do or don't do anymore. They can move on, have kids, get married, who cares? It's the one that you still love, the one that you want back, but can't have, that drives you crazy. My guilty pleasure show *Snapped* is all about this kind of love triangle, where the only way to become a couple is to kill the third point of the triangle.

Not all stories can pull off the love triangle. But even subtle flirting or wandering eyes can add tension to scenes by bringing in a third party. It's done well with Harry, Ron, and Hermione in the beginning of the *Harry Potter* series. We wonder if Harry and Hermione will ever hook up and where that will leave Ron. Eventually, we wonder if Ron will ever get the courage to ask Hermione out as the romance shifts.

Indie author Christina Benjamin does a great job of the love triangle in her *Geneva Project* series as several suitors vie for main character Geneva's attention. Her heart aches for Nova, but when she meets Kai, it seems that her affections may shift.

The thing about love triangles is making the beaus equally worthy while subtly different. The decision to "pick one" should be extremely difficult for the love interest, who will seesaw back and forth between them, along with the reader. There should be a very competitive list of characteristics they both possess that the love interest finds attractive in each of them. But ultimately, what will sway her or him, is the list of things she or he cannot live with.

For Katniss, it was the idea of leaving Peeta that hurt her the most. Gale would be fine on his own. Peeta wouldn't. She had caused him more pain than anyone else in his world. He had taught her about love and trust, things she had never known before him. Gale, on the other hand, showed a side that turned Katniss off. His ideas of "all is fair in war" went against her value of peace for the people of Panem, not to mention his idea was the one that killed her sister.

How can you wedge hurdles between your lovers by bringing in a third person? Are there scenes you can alter to provide the tension from envy and jealousy, even if just for that moment? How can outside forces make a love triangle beyond your character's control? What are they going to do about it? How far are they willing to go?

Weaving in the love triangle is a great tension builder. It can also take the hero's eyes off his goals, which can lead to all kinds of plot twists. In love, as in war, all is fair. Build in the new kid who intimidates the hero, like Ryan Rivales in my Clifton Chase novel. He shows up, and even though there is nothing going on between Clifton and Ava, he likes her. Now, she is paying attention to Ryan. She's laughing at his jokes. She's sitting at his lunch table.

This love triangle exists only in Clifton's mind, but it takes his focus off the prize, gets him into trouble, which adds tension and new plot twists to the novel. Try it for yourself. You might like what you come up with.

How can you wedge hurdles between your lovers by bringing in a third person?

_____
_____
_____ .

Are there scenes you can alter to provide the tension from envy and jealousy, even if just for that moment?

_____
_____
_____ .

How can outside forces make a love triangle beyond your character's control?

_____
_____
_____ .

What are they going to do about it, and how far are they willing to go?

_____
_____
_____ .

Chapter Twenty-Five:

Forcing Change

Have you ever found yourself reading a book and flipped through pages to jump ahead, not out of curiosity, but out of boredom? As a writer, you must pay attention to places in your novel where the action has slowed or halted, where too much dialogue transpires for too long, or where you have spent too much time in the same location or scene.

Even readers can get cabin fever, only they have the option to set your book down, jump into another story, and leave. Your characters will wait in anguish until your reader opens the book again. Some never do. With Netflix and Hulu competing for your reader's attention, the last thing you want to do is offer an out. Not even a bathroom break. Seriously.

Look for places in your story where you feel your own mind start to wander. You know if the story is not capturing your attention, as the author and creator, it won't hold your audience's attention either. Has the dialogue become redundant? Have we been through this scene already? Do we need a new setting?

This can be a great place to introduce a new character. Think about Max, the new girl in season two of *Stranger Things*, who sort of takes Eleven's place, since she is hiding out in Hopper's cabin. Max brings a new plot twist as a love triangle between Dustin and Lucas, a nemesis in the video game arcade as the new high-scorer, and a reminder to Mike that Eleven is gone as this girl tries to take her place. She is a great new character to push the story along, grow it, engage the audience with something new, and bring another awesome character to the stage: her crazy, but hot, older brother, Billy.

"Oh, Billy!"

How can you force change in your story? How do you even know where to do it? What clever ways can your hero manufacture whatever they need to alter their current path? What stories can you study to learn different ways of accomplishing this?

If your story feels stale, usually after the halfway point—the muddle in the middle—it might be because you kept going down your current story path instead of forcing a plot twist a few scenes back. Pick the spot where you feel the story lags and force a change: a death, a natural disaster, a major trickery, a needed escape. See where this change takes you and then compare it to your first version. I'm certain you won't be disappointed with the new draft, even if it doesn't look as perfect as the boring one. You'll find tension and excitement have once again returned to your plot, and you'll be back in business.

How can you force change in your story?

_____
_____
_____ .

How do you even know where to do it?

_____
_____
_____ .

What clever ways can your hero manufacture whatever they need to alter their current path?

_____
_____
_____ .

What stories can you study to learn different ways of accomplishing this?

_____
_____
_____ .

Questions to ask yourself: Has the dialogue become redundant? Have we been through this scene already? Do we need a new setting?

_____
_____
_____ .

Chapter Twenty-Six:

Motivation and Lies

Building believable characters means giving them depth and emotion. Like in real life, our characters must have driving, motivating factors that define their life choices. Sometimes, those motivations can be based in lies—the best ones often are.

The lies spoken over children shape who they become in their adult lives. "You'll never amount to anything," is a lie that if swallowed will come to pass, yet if rejected, it can become the motivation that leads to success.

Sometimes, the lies exist because we plant the seeds ourselves. Our perception twists the truth and that altered reality becomes our new reality, one by which we are motivated to change or destined to fall victim. These are qualities of humanity, which *must* be incorporated into your story world if you are ever to create characters your reader can relate to.

If a lie is so deeply ingrained that it speaks

truth, your characters will justify their actions, changing their motivation. Truly, the motivation and lies can cause them to be correct in their own mind, like in real life. However, there's a whole lot of gray between black and white.

Ender cultivated a lie planted by his brother. He is so afraid he will become a ruthless killer, like his brother, that he works tirelessly not to. Only, when push comes to shove, Ender fights back, not only to defend himself but to ensure that he will win every battle in the future. How? He destroys his enemy. His ultimate fears are realized. He has become the killer he desperately tried to avoid. Life simply happened through the filter of this lie.

Likewise, Katniss Everdeen believes the lie that she has one up on the Capitol, sneaking in the woods to hunt in District 12, selling meat in the Hob black market, and eating the berries with Peeta. She soon learns in *Catching Fire* that her lies are mere illusions and she controls nothing. Only when she can accept this truth is she ready to see the world for what it really is.

Neo from *The Matrix*.

Mr. Hillyer from *The Time Machine*.

Wolverine from *X-Men*.

The trick with writing in lies is to make the characters embrace them first, then show the choices they make because of this. It will add plot twists to your novel that you hadn't thought of in the outline. When your main character falls victim to their own lies, it's because they were forced to face those lies, no matter how hard they tried avoiding them. This means you must make your characters uncomfortable by bringing that lie to the forefront and exposing it.

A great moment in *Hunger Games* is near the end of the series, after the Capital has been taken over by Coin and President Snow is captured. Katniss meets with him in a greenhouse, and Snow points out to her that Coin had played them against each other so she could gain power and control Panem. Snow had been focused on Katniss, and she on him. Katniss didn't want to believe this truth—which also supported the lie she'd swallowed that she always had one up on Panem—but she faced it in the end when she chose to kill Coin instead of Snow. It was a very powerful sequence of events and shows that lies do motivate choices. I don't think anyone saw it coming, and that's one of the brilliant spots in this series that makes it so remarkable.

Have you built in lies to each of your characters personalities? How do these lies motivate them? Do you show the lie grow from conception to justification to acceptance as truth? What ways can you have your characters see life through the lens of their lies?

Think of some of the lies in your own life and the lives of others that have been accepted as truth. How does that affect your relationships? Pay attention to how these lies motivate people into either stagnant acceptance or aggressive resistance. Use it in your novel.

What lies have you built into each of your character's personalities?

_____

_____

_____ .

How do these lies motivate them?

_____

_____

_____ .

How do you show the lie grow from conception to justification and to acceptance as truth?

_____

_____

_____ .

What plot points can you develop as your characters see life through the lens of their lies?

_____

_____

_____ .

Chapter Twenty-Seven:

Seeing God

In your story world, you play the role of god. You are the unseen omnipotent narrator who delivers, in third- or first-person voice, the thoughts, actions, and dialogue of our characters. You are every character in your story in one way or another.

As the main character and sidekicks, you imagine how you would respond in the given situation. What would your friends do or say? As the antagonist, you may question, "What wouldn't I do in this predicament? How wouldn't I react or reply?"

Background characters may reflect those people around you, like extras in a movie or television show. They could be your neighbor, barber, teacher, or waitress. They are there to bring a deeper level of realism to your scenes.

In this way of thinking, it is appropriate to say that you are both the characters and the story god at the same time. But what happens when your characters stop listening? What do you do when you uncover something in your character that reveals a deep flaw within yourself? You can no longer control them. You no longer can predict their words or actions. It's almost as if the character has become the story god, dictating events, while you have become a whimsical character lost in the white space of your page. So what do you do? You wrestle for your power back.

In your story world, you will occasionally face a character who needs wrestling, and most often it's your own shortcoming you are facing within the characters you've created. Our characters reflect us. When they make weak choices, they are our weak choices. When they cower, it's because we cower. When they jump in without thinking, they are doing what we would do.

Our characters draw out our own imperfections, much like our children do, and unless we wrestle them by letting them see "god," our novels will never reach the potential and depth they deserve.

What ways can you wrestle with your characters? Are there permanent inflictions, either physical or emotional, that you can force on your character to get them in line? How do you resolve your own issues within the pages of your book?

Some writers take this to the extreme, using their stories to share their political or religious perspectives or discuss social issues. While this can work, you need to be careful that you aren't using the story to share your views. Weaving your world views into the story is different. The reader shouldn't feel preached to or slighted or as if the "character" is on a soapbox. Like anything else you do, the story should tell itself and not be a means for the author to make a point. If it doesn't push the story forward, it shouldn't be in the story to begin with.

If you didn't already know, Suzanne Collins was inspired to write the *Hunger Games* books when she was flipping through channels. On one station, she watched a ridiculous reality television show. On the next, war footage. She wondered how we could live in a world that had both events occurring simultaneously. She explored that topic in the creation of Panem and the Games, but she didn't dilute the story with her own politics. She made a point, not a proclamation. Your stories should read in that manner.

Writing can be a cathartic experience for not just the reader, but for you as the writer. It can be a place to share or express fears, opinions, and issues that you may not have the courage or platform to say out loud in the real world. Just be certain that if you give your character a bold voice or force them to relive your painful experiences that you are ready to face the consequences, both on the page and in your heart.

What ways can you wrestle with your characters?

_____
_____
_____ .

Are there permanent inflictions, either physical or emotional, that you can force on your character to get them in line?

_____
_____
_____ .

How do you resolve your own issues within the pages of your book?

_____
_____
_____ .

Have you written a proclamation instead of making a point? In what ways can you balance story with sharing your views?

_____
_____
_____ .

Chapter Twenty-Eight:

The Storm Before the Calm

Conflict and drama are great for fiction, but as in real life, if there is no restoration, you lose all hope. Conflicts need to be resolved, whether it be the main story problem or the minor ones along the way. These moments' drive the story and keep the reader hanging on each page. These moments allow characters to develop and grow. These moments define your story.

What thoughts were running through your character's head? What physiological responses was his body going through? Was he literally trembling? The inferred tension in the scene can be tremendous. And it should be. It is the final action before the climax.

Think of it as the storm before the calm.

The level of emotions vying for the spotlight during this moment could be unbearable if you didn't face the conflict and push through. The scene in *The Hunger Games* where Peeta and Katniss head toward the cornucopia and hear the growl of the genetically altered creatures is one of those moments. Peeta asks what the sound is and Katniss answers, "The finale." It's the storm on the horizon and it's coming fast.

The storm before the calm.

In *Back to the Future*, the final moments before Doc sends Marty back are excruciating. Doc won't listen to his future fate, the branch unplugs the cord, the car won't start, the plug separates a second time, the lighting strikes, and BAM! It all works out. Everything goes calm. The lightning stops, the winds cease, the DeLorean is gone.

The storm before the calm.

These moments must occur in your story, and not just as the climactic moment. The climax is essential but building in smaller storms that lead to calm moments will keep your reader swinging between fear and hope. It will build tension and provide relief as the story swells toward that final storm.

Have you built up your story arc to the steepest angle possible before reaching the climax? In what ways can you amp up the storm before the calm? Can you add in minor plot points that bring about tension that is resolved in restoration?

Remember, too much tension is just as bad as not enough if you don't bring it to a head. Hope drives the stories in our lives and should also drive the story you're writing. Show your characters facing many storms, and then provide both them and the reader a break in that calm period. Allow everyone to breath and gear up for what's to come.

A brilliant author who utilizes this is James Dashner in the *Maze Runner* series. I literally felt sorry for the characters as they faced trial after trial, storm after storm, making those calm moments that much sweeter and necessary.

Your characters need to be put into a position where the reader doesn't know which decision they will make at the climax moment. If you can include a life or death decision, all the better, but that doesn't match every story arch. In *Clifton Chase and the Arrow of Light*, Clifton is faced with choosing between the death of a friend or destroying the king, which is what he was brought back in time to do. If he kills the king, his friend will die. In that moment, the reader, along with Clifton, is unsure which decision he will make.

The storm before the calm.

After Clifton makes his choice, we enter a funeral march, where his friend is laid to rest. His decision has changed him, and he will return home a new person, wiser and less self-absorbed. The arrow chose him, and he carried out his mission. In the calm, on the ride home, we have a moment of peaceful reflection with Clifton during the falling action and resolution. Does your story do this? It must.

The storms are what make great fiction, but without the calms that follow, the reader would never have the chance to reflect on life lessons with the characters. Growth happens in peace, not war.

Make sure you write in quiet time for reflection.

What is the storm moment prior to the calm after the climax?

_____

_____

_____ .

What thoughts ran through your character's heads?

_____

_____

_____ .

Did you show physiological responses their bodies underwent? List 3-5.

_____

_____

_____ .

Have you built up your story arc to the steepest angle possible before reaching the climax?

_____

_____

_____ .

In what ways can you amp up the storm before the calm?

_____

_____

_____ .

Chapter Twenty-Nine:

Tell, Don't Show

I know, I know. Your jaw just dropped. What kind of a writing book is this? What writer instructs others to break the most basic of all cardinal rules, Show, Don't Tell? This one, right here.

This tricky, but it works on a few levels. Suspense books mainly follow this strategy as the reader is given information the characters aren't. Ever watched a film and yelled, "Don't go in there! The killer's waiting for you!" I know I have. This happened because I could see an important element of the story that the character could not.

In literature, it works when the reader is given information, spoken directly to them through the narrative, while remaining undisclosed to the characters. The reader has been given a glimpse into how this story might unfold.

Tell, Don't Show.

Why does this work?

Think of the many stories that use this tool successfully. We know Anakin Skywalker is flirting with the Dark Side before he slays younglings and pledges allegiance to Count Dooku. We've already seen the rise of Darth Vadar, yet we are still intrigued to watch Anakin's origin story, his twisted plight into darkness.

We know the Titanic will sink. We aren't a stranger to history. Yet, we willingly watch a movie based on the event, with full knowledge that the climax will include the boat's demise and the death of most of the passengers onboard. We know something the characters don't, and even as we witness Rose and Jack falling in forbidden love, our hearts hope theirs will be a happy ending, knowing it won't.

We even know Ariel is the real woman that the prince fell in love with and that Ursula has stolen her voice in order to pose as her. How then do we stay interested and engaged as readers?

We have all felt heartache, betrayal, and hope. We can relate to the confusion and frustration of the characters as they navigate through the story toward events that we, the reader, already know to be inevitable. It's our emotional rollercoaster, the turmoil of others that we can experience for the briefest moment before we are out of the book and back to our normal lives.

The point is to know when to tell the audience a detail in advance and when to withhold and show. Ironically, stories told from the first-person voice can know things other characters don't, which are immediately revealed to the reader through eye witness accounts, inner dialogue, and personal discovery. But the character cannot know things they do not see or hear, which means neither can the reader.

When is this the best way to tell a story? Why choose the reveal to the reader and not the character? When it builds more tension.

The tension we experience as readers when we know there is someone in the bathroom hiding behind the door with a knife is greater than the tension of walking in the bathroom with the character to take a shower. Both identical scenes take on dramatically different reactions for the reader when we know that piece of information.

The tension watching Rose and Jack fall in love, knowing they will not make it off the ship together is greater than watching a film about a boy and girl who fall in love on a big boat NOT named Titanic. It's the choice that brings more tension to the viewer. That is when you know to tell, not show.

Do you have a place in your story where the reader may feel frustrated or find themselves mad at the choices you've made because you're not sharing a crucial component? Could it be you have withheld information to make the climax a surprise? If they never finish your book, who is going to be surprised? You as the author, that's who, when you read their review on Amazon.

How can you deliver information through a Tell, Don't Show, in a way that is both believable and necessary to your characters and plot?

In a similar way, if a sequence doesn't bring tension to the story, you can tell it instead of showing it. For example, if the team decides that a car wash will bring in extra cash to pay for their entry fee to win the title, then as a reader, we don't need pages filled with the guys getting into the jeep, driving to Walmart, shopping, driving home, and getting things set up for the car wash. We may not even need to see the car wash. We might just recap, in a montage sort of way, the drive, purchase, setup, and wash, and catch back up with the story as the guys count their cash and sign up for the title competition.

Other times, you might find the whole story is built within that sequence of events, from idea to drive to store to setup to car wash. You might never get past the guys registering for the contest. That might be the goal. In that case, you would show all the mundane moments. That series of events will tell the story and reveal the characters as they head closer to the climax and grow as people.

Again, the question is which brings more tension to the story? That is when you know to tell, don't show.

It's great to string your reader along for a small while or to withhold details in order to reveal something later. But if it brings frustration, rather than nervousness, or anger, rather than hope, your audience will be upset, and never finish your novel.

Do you have a place in your story where the reader may feel frustrated or find themselves mad at the choices you've made because you're not sharing enough or a crucial component?

_____
_____
_____ .

How can you fix the places where you've withheld information to make the plot point a surprise?

_____
_____
_____ .

How can you deliver information through a Tell, Don't Show, in a way that is both believable and necessary to your characters and plot?

_____
_____
_____ .

Find places in your story that can be turned into a montage. List 3-5 of them. Ask yourself if these scenes build tension in the story or provide a delay of game to decide which to show and which to tell.

_____
_____
_____ .

Chapter Thirty:

Death and Taxes

Two things in life are certain: death and taxes.

Death is a part of life. Sometimes, our characters lose loved ones. Other times, our main characters must die. In each case, it is our job as story god to prepare the story for the tragedy in advance.

In *Star Wars Revenge of the Sith*, Padme dies while giving birth to Luke and Leah. We are heartbroken, even though we are warned this travesty would come to pass through a series of visions and dreams. Even though we know this from the original three films beginning with *A New Hope*. Chancellor Palpatine promises Anakin the power to save his loved ones from death, if he joins the Dark Side. And the very event Anakin tries to prevent— his inability to save Padme, like he couldn't save his mother—becomes the very event that ushers in Padme's untimely death. It is the force behind

Anakin's ultimate decision to join the Dark Side of the Force.

In *The Hunger Games*, Rue's death is inevitable. She reminds Katniss of Primrose, she is young and helpless, and they have formed an alliance. We know Katniss will survive the games (or at least we hope) since she's the main character. We also know that Rue won't. Funny how the story deals with both inevitables at once: *death* of the tributes in the game as *taxes*.

Sometimes, the main character must go. We know from the beginning that Harry and Voldemort will ultimately face off in a final battle to the death. Harry has a chance to win. Then, we learn that while one lives, the other must die, and we are destroyed inside. When we discover the deep-rooted connection the hero and villain share, we realize with horror that Harry will die. And when it happens, we feel helpless and empty, as if we've just lost a best friend, because, we have.

In my novella, *The Dredge*, the main character ends up sacrificing himself in the end to save the world he lives in to destroy the Regime, as he was prophesied to. It's sad to read, but even before I penned the first word, I knew Marrok would not be around for book two.

As your story god, you will have to make those hard decisions to take life from your story world. The trick is making it a result of your plot and not plotting it as a means to an end.

Does a minor character's death strengthen the main character's need to resolve their story problem? Does removing this character from the story force others to rise to the challenge? Is there a strong emotional connection established between the reader and the character, as well as the protagonist and the character for the death to even matter?

Many stories deal with death, and it makes sense, since it's one of two things in life the we must all face. Your characters should fear and respect death as the rest of us do. Show this in the story.

Spiderman broke our hearts in *End Games* when he tells Tony Stark he doesn't feel well. We know that Thanos has succeeded in wiping out half of the life in the universe. We expect it to happen when Dr. Strange tells Tony it's the only way. Yet, when half of our beloved MCU turns to ash, we are devastated. I remember that moment, not having read the comics, and I was angry for months. I couldn't believe the film ended with all my heroes dead. But Dr. Strange didn't lie, though he could've warned me about Black Widow and Iron Man. Sheesh...

Building a death scene into your story can be a powerful tool if executed properly (no pun intended). Showing "life must go on" builds character in your characters and builds a bridge between your story world and the world of your reader. We've all known death firsthand. Reliving it with our characters brings us close and allows us to heal alongside them.

How does a minor character's death strengthen the main character's need to resolve their story problem?

_____
_____
_____ .

How does removing this character from the story force others to rise to the challenge?

_____
_____
_____ .

How have you established a strong emotional connection between the reader and the character, as well as the protagonist and the minor character?

_____
_____
_____ .

If your main character dies, how does this affect the story world? Show how their sacrifice makes the world better.

_____
_____
_____ .

Chapter Thirty-One:

Symbolism and Dreams

Utilizing dreams is one of my favorite tools as an author. In dreams, you can foreshadow and reveal traits, through the character's subconscious, that build plot. Dreams can add layers and dimensions through symbolism and imagery in a way that no other writing device can. And the truth is revealed to the characters in different ways, viewed through their own lens of lies, misconceptions, and judgments.

Harry Potter has dreams of things that are happening in Voldemort's world, through his eyes or sometimes his snake's, Nagini. These dreams are discovered to be Voldemort's consciousness, that Harry can access as one of the villains horcruxes.

In my novel *Exposure*, Tember has visions of his parents through dreams that provide more insight and clues as to their whereabouts. These dreams are essential to his journey and reveal future events and plot points that push him forward.

In crafting dreams, you can either inject them during the first draft writing or sprinkle them in afterward to lay a foundation for events in your story. The dreams need to be symbolic and hazy, as they are in real life, for the characters to believe they hold merit. When your main character has dreams, he should keep hold of them and work to figure out their meaning or find a connection to them at a later point in the narrative. They should not be instruction manuals or so obvious that your reader doesn't buy them.

Dreams can also work against the main character to build more tension and story problems. In Clone Wars, Anakin has dreams about his mother's death, which come to pass. This is a great red herring, in a way, that leads him and the reader into a trick in *The Phantom Menace*. During the third episode of the Star Wars series, Anakin begins to have dreams of Padme dying in childbirth. Based off his earlier visions of his mother's death, we and he believe this to be truth. His dreams have already come to pass once. Why wouldn't they come to pass again?

These dreams push him to learn more about the Dark Side of the Force, which apparently has lessons in saving loved ones from death. Perfect! That's just what Anakin needs to make sure his dream doesn't come to pass. What happens next? His dreams cause the death of Padme in childbirth because he is so intent on stopping it that he joins the bad guys, kills kids, and accuses Padme of betraying him. He is so blinded by his own dreams and desperation to prevent them from coming to pass, that he injures Padme and she dies in childbirth.

I don't think Anakin would have been so set on believing Padme was going to die if his first dream about his mother hadn't come to pass. This was great writing. The use of dreams in one film led to Anakin finding his mother and bringing her home. The use of dreams in the next film fed to Anakin a list of lies that altered his life forever.

As you work through your manuscript, are there places you can add symbolic dreams to foreshadow the story's climax? Can you take something literal and make it vaguer through picture meaning or definitions? Have you considered incorporating a dream dictionary to take the dreams you have already built into your story and give them more cryptic meaning?

If you can use dreams as an unreliable narrator, as done in Star Wars, do it! The more tension and false motivations you can bring into your story, the harder the hero's journey will become. And the harder the journey, the more we will love them as readers, remembering them off the page, and immortalizing them in literature.

As you work through your manuscript, are there any places you can add symbolic dreams to foreshadow the story's climax?

_____

_____

_____ .

Where can you take something literal and make it vaguer through picture meaning or definitions? Give 3-5 examples.

_____

_____

_____ .

Using a dream dictionary, where can you take the dreams you have already built into your story and give them more cryptic meaning?

_____

_____

_____ .

Are you able to craft dreams as unreliable narrators? Show some ways you could incorporate dreams into a series that are right sometimes and wrong other times.

_____

_____

_____ .

Chapter Thirty-Two:

Inference Behind Scenes

Say a homeless guy tells you he has nowhere to go as a category four hurricane heads toward the coast, located a few feet from the bench he calls home. Do you need to know what happened to him in order to determine he's homeless or can you infer by his appearance and dialogue that something in his past set him on a path to live at that beach bench?

In your story world, much should occur off the pages, before the moment when your story starts. Even if it's not found in the text, readers will figure it out. They will still get it. They don't have to be told everything. For some reason, authors feel the need to spell out things in the narrative that they describe in the dialogue, especially plot twists.

Sarah worried that Ron was the killer because of his watch. "You're the killer, aren't you? You're wearing Mr. Ferguson's watch"

Did we need both? Couldn't we discover the

reveal in the dialogue alongside the killer? Telling it first in narrative, then in dialogue takes away the tension. It's like telling someone "God Bless You" before they sneeze.

Inference is a much better way to share.

Sarah stared at Ron's watch. "You're the killer, aren't you?"

This inference that Sarah discovered something when she looked at Ron's watch is clear through her narrative description and dialogue to follow. The reader doesn't need it spelled out. Seriously, we don't. Let the reader figure it out a hair quicker than the characters, and they will think you're a genius.

Inference builds frustration and motivation into your plot. This will allow you to suddenly have a group of characters plotting murder without the reader blinking an eye. Too often plot points occur that feel convenient or surprising because they *don't* make sense, but not because they *can't*. The author failed to establish a few moments in the narrative to frame what was happening behind the scenes. The reader would have filled in the rest, through inference, filtered by their own life experiences.

In *Maze Runner*, the opposite is true. We believe something happened prior to Thomas awakening in the maze, even if no one can remember. As readers, we don't need all the exposition up front. We can infer that something happened in the real world and that we will eventually figure it out. After all, someone had to give birth to all those boys.

Leave places in the story for your reader to infer what will happen, what has happened, and what is happening. Bread crumbs can lead the way. Photos can show where you've been. Don't be surprised if your reader reads into things you hadn't intended. That's okay. If they arrive at the same point in the story, it doesn't matter.

Perspective is built off past experiences, personal biases, religious and political views, and economic or social status. Keep these things in mind as you build your story. If the inference isn't possible for multiple people groups, then you may have to tell more in the narrative by stringing together a few concrete details.

In your story, have you given too many details? Have you provided side story that doesn't keep the story flowing naturally? Where can you remove information, relying on the intellect of the reader to fill in the blanks?

Humans share many feelings and reactions. Many are simply variations, which grow in scale as a direct result of wounds and lies. Envy becomes jealousy becomes hatred becomes vengeance becomes murder. If you give a few details of a jealous character and then later, show them plotting revenge, your reader can infer the decline in emotion. They can decide the character is suffering from envy. An anxious character can easily develop paranoia with time, and if you show them reacting out of fear and desperation, the reader can infer the rest.

Try observing characters in movies or

television you know well. Decide which core emotion they exhibit, then list the varying degrees associated with it. Where are they in the spectrum? Where can they go from here? How can you show one or two details to let the reader infer the rest? Remember, the greater the spiral from normal, the steeper the climb back to emotional equilibrium and the more tension you will build into your narrative.

In your story, where have you given too many details?

_____
_____
_____ .

Pick a story thread. List 3-5 of the ways you've provided concrete details your reader can string together.

_____
_____
_____ .

How can you remove excessive information, relying on the intellect of the reader to fill in the blanks?

_____
_____
_____ .

List some of the emotions you've given your main characters that are rooted in deeper emotions for the reader to infer.

_____
_____
_____ .

Chapter Thirty-Three:

Subplots

Every great plot has equally great subplots. The 'B' story, if you will. Some are even so amazing that spinoffs featuring these stories can result. Most times, they are based off profound characters such as *X-Men's* Wolverine, *Pitch Black's* Riddick, and *Star Wars'* Anakin Skywalker.

In *Stranger Things*, the main story line is finding Will. Within that, there are several subplots to include the love triangle with Nancy, Steve, and Jonathan, the disappearance of Barb, the introduction of Elle, the demidogs, the Upside Down, and the total annihilation of Hawkins. The sub-stories keep the plot moving forward, because just looking for Will isn't enough.

In *Harry Potter*, the books are riddled (see what I did there?) with subplots. The story problem is basically the fight against Voldemort, but each book has its own additional set of problems and new cast list. *Supernatural* also includes subplots and storylines, even including alternate universes within the universe.

In your stories, it is crucial to weave in subplots that affect your secondary character's lives and give them the motivation they need to organically produce their decisions. If they have no believable lives of their own, they will come across as fixtures whose only purpose is to assist or interfere with the main character's plight.

Without Mike crushing on Elle, or Nancy trying to pick between Jonathan and Steve while dealing with Barb's disappearance, they would only be people in the background helping Joyce find her son.

Without Cas and his mission to fight the angels or Crowley and his plight to strengthen his position as the king of Hell, Sam and Dean would be humanized versions of the Scooby Doo Mystery Team, solving whodunit mysteries involving paranormal beings. Would still be a cool show as its original inception of a legend and lore buddy cop show, but these subplots really kick up the series and have allowed it to live more than a decade onscreen.

Who are your book's primary secondary characters? What motivates them? Do they have a subplot that **needs** (keyword: *needs*) to be shared in order to reveal something about the character that the reader *must* know in order to move the story forward?

In *Prisoner of Azkaban*, Hermione has an

entire subplot which feeds the main plot line. She is given a time-turner to all ow her to be in two classes at once. She has her own story offscreen, her own goals, and her own means of achieving them. The brilliance of this subplot is that this time-turner becomes the solution to solve the main story plot. That is great writing, when a sub-story crosses a main vein, and the plot is stronger because of it.

There's a great difference between backstory and subplot. While sometimes they are one in the same, the backstory is usually an enhancement to the literary experience while the subplot is integral. And, if done correctly, you could create a subplot that is so phenomenal that it carries its own storyline.

Who are your book's primary secondary characters?

_____

_____

_____ .

What motivates your secondary characters? Show 3-5 examples.

_____

_____

_____

_____

_____ .

Within each secondary character's subplot, what **needs** to be shared to reveal something about the character the reader *must* know?

_____

_____

_____ .

Chapter Thirty-Four:

Ups & Downs

In a perfect world, we find safety in the belief that if we follow the rules, good things happen. We eat right, exercise, pay our taxes, and follow the golden rule expecting life to be smooth and the "Universe" to reward us for our good deeds.

In the same way, we expect the bad guys to pay for their wrongs, for justice to prevail, for the consequence to fit the crime. But life doesn't always work that way. Non-smokers get lung cancer. Drunk drivers kill high schoolers. Famous singers die in plane crashes.

When the characters in your book face unfair consequences, the reader feels enraged. They will demand justice. The story universe is imbalanced and must be fixed.

Dorothy finally meets the Wizard. She followed the Good Witch's rules. Stayed on the path. Offered to help her new friends. The Wicked Witch of the East followed her the whole way. Trees tried to attack her when she picked their fruit. Poppies put her to sleep. But she perseveres. She reaches the Emerald City, with her friends by her side. Only when she knocks on the door and is announced, the Wizard says, "Go away."

We can't believe it. Dorothy did everything she was supposed to. This, by the way, is called a False Victory, and it happens at the halfway point of the story. It's the moment where you think your hero has succeeded, only it's their first blow to becoming the hero the story has called them to be.

If the Wizard had whisked Dorothy home, she would have found her problems waiting for her. Things may have been okay for a while, but Dorothy would have become dissatisfied again with the world around her, because she never grew in Oz. Instead, she was forced to face her fears after following the Wizard's request, and she realized the power to go home was inside her all along. And more importantly, she taught the world that there's no place like home.

Characters rising and falling as a result of the decisions of others builds tremendous, genuine sympathy from the reader. We have all been betrayed and wrongfully accused, so we can easily relate to this feeling and to our expectations of eventual retribution. The truth will be revealed.

Spiderman gets superpowers. He plays around with them until he figures things out, and he thinks he's fit to save the world. But then, the villain puts him in his place. He is not as strong as he thinks.

He is not as super as he thinks. He must go through the trials after the halfway point to get to his dark moment. From there, he can enter Act III and find a way to save the day, usually with the help of his friends. In the end, though, he'll ultimately face the villain alone, but by then he'll have found the strength he needs.

It's these ups and downs from scene to scene that build character, in your character, and sympathy from your reader. You must show these elements. Your protagonist must be pushed into her journey, discover her powers, face a false victory or false defeat, and fight her way to near death. Then, when we think all is lost, she'll get lifted by a team of friends, find the inner strength she needs to face the enemy, save the day, and be victorious by the end.

Can you supply a scene in your story where your hero is wrongfully accused and punished for no reason? How does he react? Does she patiently wait for the truth to be uncovered or go down kicking and screaming?

In some novels, this is the basis of the entire plot. A wrongfully accused hero spends his journey proving his innocence. Weave in failures and compound the accusation. Plant evidence that points fingers at your heroine. Just remember that even when the world looks bleak, and darkness reigns, the reader can always find hope...in the next chapter.

Can you supply a scene in your story where your hero is wrongfully accused and punished for no reason?

_____

_____

_____ .

How does he or she react?

_____

_____

_____ .

Do they patiently wait for the truth to be uncovered or go down kicking and screaming?

_____

_____

_____ .

Show how you followed the structure to hit your beats to maximize the ups and downs throughout the story? List the beats on a separate page if needed.

_____

_____

_____ .

Chapter Thirty-Five:

New Characters in the Middle

Each story has a basic beginning, middle, and end; an Act I, Act II, and Act III. The beginning introduces the characters, their world, and the story problem. We see them in their safe place, learning their powers or starting their journey to become a hero.

The middle section of the story is the place of the character's low points. They are beat up and tired, if you're a good author, facing a place where they are abandoned and alone, probably ready to throw in the towel. But they won't.

Act III sums it all up. Brings the story to a close and shows us that our main character is worthy of being remembered as a hero.

Characters have purpose. They aren't haphazardly introduced for no reason, nor are they all introduced in the first chapter. Plot twists occur by the pressure these new characters place on our hero. If your hero could solve the problems on their own, we wouldn't be able to relate to them. Your reader needs to know there's a place for them in your story. If your hero is self-sufficient, it makes us feel bad about ourselves because we are not self-sufficient. We need to imagine ourselves in the story, helping the hero, like Samwise when Frodo falls on his face.

In *Ender's Game*, Petra Arkanian is introduced in the middle of the story. She impacts Ender's next moves, trains him in the battle room, and provides the friendship he needs to succeed. If she hadn't been in Salamander, Ender's story would have paused because Bonzo wouldn't allow him to train. Petra provided Ender with the tools he needed to grow as a character and to get prepared for the next plot point in the story: the false victory.

Although we meet Rue early in the *Hunger Games* during the "fun and games" section, it is the friendship she provides and ally she becomes for Katniss that matter. Rue gives Katniss the determination she needs to press on till the ending and the idea to cut down the tracker jacker nest to escape the District 1 and 2 Tributes. Rue brings outlying Panem together when Katniss honors her death, something that does not go unnoticed in the districts. Rue triggers the first of Katniss's unintentional rebellion against the Capital.

What new characters need to be introduced into your story to push your main character to the ending? Do you have essential information that needs to be delivered to the main character and the reader? How can you bring in the perfect new character to deliver the message?

New characters can also cause problems for the main character, whether on purpose or accident. Max from *Stranger Things* causes tension in the group for a variety of reasons. Two of the boys like her and the third resents her for taking Eleven's place, none of which Max has control over. In the *Wizard of Oz*, the Wizard himself shows up at the midpoint of the story and causes all kinds of trouble for Dorothy. He was supposed to solve her problem and tell her how to go home. Instead, he cowardly commands her to go to the Wicked Witch's house and steal her broomstick.

New characters are great to keep the middle fresh, give the main character hope or conflict, and push the story toward climax. Sometimes, they are so remarkable they become staples in the series or even go on to star in stories of their own.

What new characters need to be introduced into your story to push your main character to the ending?

_____
_____
_____ .

Do you have essential information that needs to be delivered to the main character and the reader? Give 3-5 examples.

_____
_____
_____
_____
_____ .

How can you bring in the perfect new character to deliver the message?

_____
_____
_____ .

Have you brought in a midpoint character who causes problems for the hero, whether on purpose or unintentional? Describe them.

_____
_____
_____ .

Chapter Thirty-Six:

Anticipating the Foreshadowed

Earlier we discussed the power of foreshadow. You can deliver it through dreams, prophecies, song, or magic, depending on your story. What might happen is you, the writer, forgets these brilliantly placed moments in your story, never to return to or act on what you promised.

It's an easy mistake to make. You've set up this scene and then the story happens. You forget and move on to the end. I recommend a list as you write, where you can add these nuggets you've foreshadowed to make sure you eventually come back to them.

Imagine if the mockingjay pin Katniss received in the Hob never meant anything and never got mentioned again. What if Tony Stark hadn't mentioned he had everything he needed in the world and that creating a time machine could jeopardize it all, then nothing happened to him. We knew in that scene that Tony was going to die. At least, that was the foreshadow set up in the dialogue.

It can be a simple phrase, a movement, a street sign that implies something from this moment will show itself again later in the story. It can be a century old prophecy, a recurring dream, a psychic prediction that leads the hero on his quest. Imagine if it never came to pass. How confused and disappointed would you be as a reader?

It's important that you follow through with your promises, including what you foreshadow. You made a promise with your reader that you are expected to deliver on. This is true of many aspects of your story, including the genre and cover art (believe it or not), so make sure what you say is gonna happen, really happens.

Have you clearly shown your foreshadowed events coming to pass in your story? Did you include enough supporting data through scenes earlier in the book to make the outcome believable? Is there a pattern of moments that you can go back through and weave tighter together through threads of foreshadow?

Those foreshadowed segments should be subtle, but their impact should be glaring. Think of ways in which this tool is used in stories you love. Would the event have held as much punch without the foreshadow leading to it?

Characters can foreshadow other characters as well. *Holes* is a great example of this, with Madame

Zeroni and her curse placed on the Yelnats's family. The entire story is woven around this curse and its impact in Stanley's life. Every bad thing is blamed on the fact that his no-good-dirty-rotten-pig-stealing-great-great-grandfather never brought Madame Zeroni up the mountain like he'd promised. This is some seriously subtle foreshadowing. When Stanley carries Zero up the mountain, we get the connection. It's brilliant. We consider *Holes* a classic and find ourselves watching it for the millionth time, to see that beautifully woven foreshadow come to pass.

The role of Gollum in Frodo's quest, as foreshadowed by Gandalf, plays out when Frodo and Gollum battle over the ring on Mount Doom, even unto death. Gandalf warns of the ring's power and tells the story of the Stoor Hobbit named Smeagol, who was corrupted by the ring and became a wretched creature. Throughout the story, we slowly see the deterioration of Frodo, who is becoming more and more like Smeagol as the ring digs deeper into his soul. We wonder if Gandals's story is a foreshadow of things to come and, more importantly, if Frodo will be able to overcome the power of the ring.

Professor Quirrel's "obsession" with Harry Potter seems fanatical, until we understand he is Lord Voldemort's vessel in *The Sorcerer's Stone*. In *Twilight*, Stephenie Myer used Bella's gift to subconsciously block out Edward from reading her mind, and to form a shield against powers when she becomes a vampire in *Breaking Dawn*.

Subtle, but powerful. That's what makes great

foreshadowing. Just remember to show the end result or else your reader will leave wondering what happened.

Have you clearly shown your foreshadowed events coming to pass in your story?

_____

_____

_____ .

Did you include enough supporting data through scenes earlier in the book to make the outcome believable?

_____

_____

_____ .

Is there a pattern of moments that you can go back through and weave tighter together through threads of foreshadow?

_____

_____

_____ .

Would the event have held as much punch without the foreshadow leading to it?

_____

_____

_____ .

Chapter Thirty-Seven:

The Red Herring

The Red Herring is a great literary device used to force attention off the central issue and onto something else. The first thing to figure out is why use a Red Herring at all? What's the purpose to pushing the story forward if the literary device serves the story? These are great questions, and like always the answer is simple: tension.

If you can send the reader on a rabbit trail while maintaining control of your story, the Red Herring will enhance your novel. It is not an easy thing to do. You have to know the journey yet set up an alternate road for the reader to travel down, while still staying in the main story thread and not losing their place. Seriously. I'm exhausted just writing that.

In *The Da Vinci Code,* Dan Brown leads the reader to believe Bishop Aringarosa is the villain, but he serves as the Red Herring to throw the focus off of the real antagonists.

In *Great Expectations*, Charles Dickens vividly leads the reader to believe that Pip's benefactor is the eccentric and wealthy Miss Havisham. We'd bet on it! But she's the Red Herring meant to misdirect the reader's attention away from the escaped convict whom Pip aided, as a small boy, to flee the police.

In any Scooby-Doo Mysteries (yep, I went there) the success of each story is following clues that point the gang toward an innocent, yet likely suspect, only to discover it was someone they probably already knew... who would have gotten away with it if it hadn't been for those meddling kids.

When used well, it works. It's an essential device in cozy mysteries or whodunits. You want the reader to think someone committed the crime when all along it's been the butler with the candlestick in the parlor. However, when an author intentionally leads the reader off the trail for the sole purpose of shock value, with no deepening of the plot or character development, the reader will get mad.

Intentional deceit is never well-received. Not in real life and not in fiction. It will leave your reader feeling like they've wasted their time and guarantee a miserable review of your book. Point the finger off center stage, use a sleight of hand to focus their attention elsewhere, and when they've taken the bait, you present the big reveal. That's how a great magician does it. They get you focused on something unimportant while the important action happens somewhere else, where you're not looking. I should know. My neighbor is Magic Bob.

Are there places in your story where a Red Herring will enhance your story? Have you added a Red Herring to serve a purpose instead of the plot? What ways can you alter that? Look at some stories that have successfully implemented the Red Herring and those that haven't. Can you list why you feel some worked while others didn't?

For me, when I feel like I've been dragged all over the story world when everything I needed was right in scene one, I feel frustrated, unless the author provides a great reason. Books such as *Alice in Wonderland*, *The Wizard of Oz*, and the Underland Chronicles book 6 by Suzanne Collins titled *Gregor and the Curse of the Warmbloods*, utilize the Red Herring in an exceptional fashion.

These books take the character on a wonderful adventure in search of answers, be it to find home or find a way to save home. Only the truth was right in front of them. The Red Herring *is* the adventure, because the answer was back home on the banks by the river, in Kansas, or in the Kingdom within the Underland. The adventure was necessary for the character to find strength and to grow, something they wouldn't have experienced without the Red Herring adventure. And it worked because it was an organic component of the plot and not something forced into the story to lead the reader astray and teach the characters a lesson.

Practice writing a few red herrings into your story scenes and see how it works. Share them with others to find out how they react as you stretch yourself as a writer and write outside of your comfort zone.

Name at least one place in your story where a Red Herring will enhance it.

_____
_____
_____ .

Have you added a Red Herring to serve a purpose other than the plot? What makes you think so?

_____
_____
_____ .

What ways can you alter the story line, so the red herring is essential to the plot for the character's growth?

_____
_____
_____ .

Can you list why you feel some stories with red herrings worked while others didn't?

_____
_____
_____ .

Chapter Thirty-Eight:

The Darkest Night

The darkest night moment in the story is where things are at their worst for our hero, forcing them into the third act and climax. There is no good choice. Death awaits at every turn. The ideal darkest night moment falls upon our characters. They are forced to make a choice, the lesser of two evils, knowing their fate is not secure and knowing they are walking into the enemy's camp.

What is Dorothy Gale's darkest night moment in *The Wizard of Oz*? She's reached the Emerald City, met the Wizard, and is forced to retrieve the broomstick of the Wicked Witch of the West if she ever wants to return to Kansas. The flying monkeys come. Dorothy is separated from her friends, but Toto escapes. Then, a crystal ball sends word from Aunt Em that pushes Dorothy over the edge. She agrees to give up the ruby slippers. This means her death. Better to go willing. However, the magic backfires and the witch is angered, unable to remove the ruby slippers as long as Dorothy's alive. The hourglass counts away one piece of sand at a time, the remaining seconds of her life before the witch kills her to take her slippers. Every direction leads to death. The darkest night moment. Then, her friends arrive to save her.

Act III has begun.

In *The Hunger Games*, Katniss is betrayed by Peeta, stung by tracker jackers, and then Rue is killed in her arms. She has died on the inside and she realizes she is going to die in the arena. Her darkest night moment has arrived. But then, the commentator explains a change in the rules. Two tributes from the same district can co-win the games. She must find Peeta.

Act III has begun.

It's so important that your main character is pressed to this moment where all is lost and defeat (or death) awaits at every turn. This is the place where they can rise, at long last, to become the hero we, as the reader, have always known they would become, able to fulfill their calling. It takes fire to forge a blade. Our characters need the fire to be so hot they can't breathe. They must feel completely defeated and at a loss, hopeless and abandoned, to find the strength to face the villain in the end and save the day.

Have you knocked down your main character enough to remove their options and leave them hopeless? In what ways can you add more elements of defeat and despair? Can you isolate them? Can you bring them to Death's door at every turn? Can you make them desperate?

I would recommend an in-depth study of books and movies you know very well to find and analyze the main character's darkest night moment. What decisions were made? What led them there? What choices remained and what were the consequences of making those choices? By reviewing well-written moments that force characters into the third act, you'll better construct your own story elements and force your character to face their darkest night moment.

And here's a final tip: in this dark place, the character is forced alone with their fatal flaw, the element that paints in the theme. Dorothy sees Aunt Em and then...just wants to go home, realizing family is more important than anything else. This is the opposite of her worldview in scene one.

Katniss realizes she can't protect those she loves, helpless from the terrors of the Capital, no matter how hard she tries, and that she needs others to survive. This is the opposite of her worldview in scene one.

Remember, dig deep and weave those themes and flaws into your character's need to reach their goal. This darkest night moment is where your character's vulnerability is exposed, yet they still choose to fight. It's their final step to becoming a hero.

Have you knocked down your main character enough to remove their options and leave them hopeless?

_____
_____
_____ .

In what ways can you add more elements of defeat and despair? Can you isolate them? Can you bring them to Death's door at every turn? Can you make them desperate?

_____
_____
_____
_____
_____ .

Analyze the main character's darkest night moment. What decisions were made? What led them there? What choices remained and what were the consequences of making those choices?

_____
_____
_____
_____
_____ .

Chapter Thirty-Nine:

The Climax

This is why we read, isn't it? This is what every story leads to: the climax.

We see it in series, the overarching story line that's resolved once and for all in the final climax of the last book.

Maze Runner.

Harry Potter.

The Hunger Games.

It's easier to gloss over this moment and underwrite it then to indulge in the tension and release. It's not hard to write a scene where a woman walks to her mailbox to check her mail but try writing the scene where she opens the door to check the mail and her deployed husband stands on the doorstep. Writing tension is difficult. Writing the mundane is simple.

As the reader waits on bated breath, we realize we are at the climax. The story can go either way, good or bad. Life or death. Clean or messy. Happily ever after or not so much. Before you pen your first word, this moment needs to be decided. You should know if the story will end in a win, lose, or draw. It's crucial, because when you arrive here, it will help you to write the tension, pain, and joy this scene needs to be truly effective and bring your story to its highest point of dramatic tension.

In *Hunger Games*, this is the moment when Katniss holds out the Nightlock berries and she and Peeta countdown to their own deaths. The abovementioned questions flit through our minds while we read the book or watch the movie. Will they do it? Will they die? Will we make it? Will something rescue them?

In *The Wizard of Oz*, this is when the hot air balloon lifts and soars of its own accord, leaving Dorothy forever stranded in Oz. We quickly learn that Dorothy has the power to return to Oz in her slippers, and for a moment, we wonder if she will stay or if she will go. Is the Wizard coming back? How?

In *The Maze Runner*, we see this when Thomas plans the jump, and everyone knows it will kill them too. Will they make it? Will they live? What's on the other side of that wall? Is it worse than what they're leaving? How many will die?

As you reach your story's climax, don't rush things. Give the reader that sense of hopelessness, insurmountable odds, and no way out. Get them to the point where they need a miracle, and then rush the reader through the fear, the unknown, the chaos you've created until, breathless, we all reach the other side.

Have you made your climax too weak? What other obstacles could you add in leading up to it? Have you made things too easy for your characters? Where can you amp up the tension and the stakes to create a more impactful climax?

By studying other stories, you will notice those places just before the climax where you are uncertain if the hero will make it or not. Learn from them. Begin to build in those same moments that will cause your reader to wonder and fear the same things.

In what ways have you made your climax weak?

_____

_____

_____ .

What other obstacles could you add leading up to it?

_____

_____

_____ .

How have you made things too easy for your characters?

_____

_____

_____ .

Where can you amp up the tension and the stakes to create a more impactful climax?

_____

_____

_____ .

Chapter Forty:

It's never too late

As an author your task is to give your reader enough information to reveal the story as you go, and nothing more. That doesn't mean you withhold valuable plot or character development to create a surprise ending. But it does mean that sometimes a story or character may be presented in one light while all the while something entirely different is going on.

The best example of this technique is the movie *The Sixth Sense* by M. Night Shyamalan. If you don't know it, stop reading this book and go watch that film—though you'll have to watch it a second time after you finish. Trust me. It's brilliant filmmaking. Your view of the main and supporting character and their view of the world shifts so dramatically, that you are literally watching two complete movies, one with one expectation and the second completely different.

In storytelling, it's never too late for a character reveal that shifts the plot. In fact, it's why we read. But this shift has to serve the story, not be added in for effect. Otherwise, we won't be happy readers.

When Lucas reveals that Darth Vader is Luke's and Leah's father in *The Empire Strikes Back*, it changes everything; so much so that the series goes back to the beginning in the 2000s to show Vader's decline from Anakin Skywalker to the ruthless villain just before the birth of his twins. The first time we heard the line, "I am your father," it changed us forever, at least if you're a *Star Wars* geek like I am.

In the Harry Potter franchise, we are flabbergasted when Dumbledore reveals that he knew all along that Harry would have to die one day to defeat Voldemort and amazed at Dumbledore's willingness to sacrifice his "son" for the greater good. Then, we discover how Snape shares not only a love for Harry's mother, but has made a sacrificial promise to care for and protect Harry from the shadows. It's completely unexpected and so powerful that it shifts our perspective of these characters forever. Now *that's* good storytelling!

The point? It's never too late.

In your story, have you built up to character and plot twists that surprise the reader? Do these moments happen organically from the plot or have you developed a plot to serve the surprise?

It's very important you don't write a whole story to serve a "Wow!" moment at the end. That's a mistake many beginning writers fall into and the story can tend to read like a Scooby-Doo Mystery.

When I wrote my novel *Dreadlands*, I knew a couple things. At that time I wrote as a Pantster, so the beginning and end were clear, the middle a big muddle following the characters and writing down what happened. The things I knew would happen at the end were (*spoiler alert) a huge, epic battle between man and beast and that the person I had worked the reader to believe to be the villain was not the actual villain at all. While that character was bad, they were a puppet on a string that led to an even bigger and badder villain. I wanted my own Vadar-Palpatine moment with the same hierarchy in place. And it worked. Many readers were shocked to learn who the real villain was and how they related to characters in the story and the prophecy.

Build in moments that act as clues for the steadfast reader, but don't appear so obvious that they give themselves away. Then, when your story leads to the big reveal, your reader will think back upon the breadcrumbs you've scattered for them and feel satisfied. They will either piece it together before your reveal and feel awesome that they were right or realize that they knew it all along and can't believe they didn't piece it together earlier. Either way, they will not feel shocked because you have left dots to connect.

There's nothing worse than figuring out a whole story halfway through because the author planted obvious clues to push the story toward a planned, "surprise" ending. Instead, use your story to move the plot along while you find those threads you've already created. Weave them together to produce that surprise ending no one will see coming, not even you!

Remember, it's never too late.

In your story, where have you built up to character and plot twists that surprise the reader?

_____
_____
_____ .

Do these moments happen organically from the plot or have you developed a plot to serve the surprise?

_____
_____
_____ .

How have you left an adequate bread crumb trail to lead the reader toward one outcome, before snatching it away to show another?

_____
_____
_____ .

Chapter Forty-One:

Reconciliation

In fiction, as in life, humans seek reconciliation, peace, and harmony. While we are not always willing or able to achieve it in our real lives, story provides the perfect place for us to experience the warm fuzzies at the end. It's one of the reasons why we love story so much. Overall, no one likes uneasiness, discomfort, turmoil, or chaos. Mankind's not built that way. Enter reconciliation—it's a beautiful thing.

We see it in great stories.

A Christmas Carol.

The Wizard of Oz.

It's A Wonderful Life.

We witness the act within stories, when Frodo and Sam make amends. In *How the Grinch Stole Christmas,* when the Whos and the Grinch reconcile and forgive. In *The Phantom Tollbooth*, when Milo reconciles two kingdoms: Digitopolis (numbers) and Dictionopolis (words).

Building a scene where characters or kingdoms reconcile is no easy task. The further apart they grow and the least likely the possibility for future interaction, the greater the end result. Time doesn't heal all wounds. Sometimes, they fester.

We love Ebenezer Scrooge, not because he is fair to his employees, charitable with his great excess of wealth, or cordial at family dinners. Those are expected social norms. What pulls at our heartstrings is watching him behave in this manner after we saw what a jerk he was, not only in the present, but also in the past and future. His wide-reaching transformation makes the reconciliation more dramatic. There is so much opposition between who he was and who he becomes in the end. It is this deep, vast cavern of difference that makes us love *A Christmas Carol* nearly 200 years later.

One of my favorites is *Groundhog Day*. Bill Murray and Andie McDowell are brilliant together. In this film, Phil, a pompous a-hole of a guy, finds himself stuck in a small town for an endless timeframe as Groundhog Day repeats every morning. He follows the pattern of storytelling to a "t" and it's why this film still makes me cry at the end every time I watch it. Phil is confused when he wakes up to the same day, but then, he moves through the fun and games stage until it's not fun anymore. He can't win Rita's heart, no matter how hard he tries.

Then, Phil decides to die, over and over again, but he still wakes up on Groundhog Day. What's left? He begins to help people. He helps a lot of people and stops thinking about himself first. He enters into a state of complacency, almost satisfaction in his new existence. And it's when he reconciles with his place, lack of control, and humility that the day breaks and it turns to February 3rd. Phil spent 12,403 days (33 years and 358 days) stuck in Groundhog Day. It took that much time for him to find reconciliation, and in the end, he gets the girl too.

Have you built in drama and hurts that are left unaddressed? Have time and distance compounded these feelings to make the drama larger than it really is? Have you presented the appearance of no possible solutions? Good. You've set up the perfect storm for a dynamic reconciliation.

How have you built in drama and pain left unchecked?

_____

_____

_____ .

Show how time and distance compound these feelings to make the drama larger than life.

_____

_____

_____ .

In what ways have you presented the appearance of no possible solutions?

_____

_____

_____ .

Share the elements in the scenes where your character finds reconciliation. How can you draw out more emotion?

_____

_____

_____ .

Chapter Forty-Two:

Setting Up the Sequel

One great thing about being a writer is leaving open strings that lead to book two. The trick to writing sequels is to end the first book as a standalone with a complete and satisfying end for your reader. You don't have to clear up every story problem presented. You want to leave some hanging threads on the tapestry of story you've woven, in order to leave the possibility of writing your sequel.

Setting up the sequel requires a clear resolution of the story problem presented in book one. You cannot end book one on a cliffhanger in attempts to string the reader along and force them to read your sequel to finish your story. Unless you are striving for 1-star reviews. You will lose your reader's trust and they will hate you if you don't give them an ending that completes the book they've read. They must feel like the story problem presented in the beginning is tied up and answered by "the end" of book one.

With this said, you can and should leave some details unresolved to continue the overarching story problem that connects the books in a series. *The Hunger Games, Maze Runner,* and *Harry Potter*, each demonstrate the careful balance of closing the story problem with a clear resolution while keeping a larger problem unsolved until the final book in the series.

The Capital is still in charge by the end of book one.

Thomas and his crew still don't know the reasons for the maze by the end of book one.

Harry Potter has not defeated Voldemort by the end of book one.

If you are planning a sequel, did you end your first book with a satisfying close? Did you solve the current story problem, or did you end on a cliffhanger to secure book two?

If book one requires book two to be complete, you haven't done your job as an author and have broken the unspoken contract with your reader. Your job is to present and resolve a problem within the book's pages. Not every problem, but that particular book's problem. Instead, you have strung the reader along for 300 or so pages only to smack a big "To Be Continued" in their faces.

The only time you can pull this off is the transition between book two and book three, or the second to last book and the last book if your series is greater than a trilogy. Your reader is invested by that point. In fact, in most cases, book two should end on a hopeless note. You almost require a book three after book two when it ends on a low point.

The Empire Strikes Back.

Catching Fire.

The Scorch Trials.

These three series have an "all is lost" ending to book (or movie) two that continues in book (or movie) three to close the series. Your reader is invested by the end of book two and willing to accept your "To Be Continued" sign.

As an example, *The Hunger Games* trilogy didn't need a book two or three. We had a clear close and were satisfied with the ending. But at the end of book two, we were left on a cliffhanger and had to continue to book three if we wanted to know how the overall story ended. The formula is executed perfectly by Suzanne Collins.

In the same sense, Harry Potter has the same effect. By the end of the *Sorcerer's Stone*, Harry has found the villain and accepted his place in his new wizarding world. The overarching problem with Voldemort is mentioned, but not even slightly resolved. However, if there had never been a second book in this series, I wouldn't have left feeling duped. I would have felt satisfied that the story ended with a complete tale and moved on to read something else. Of course, I wouldn't want to live in that universe where *Harry Potter* was a standalone novel, but you get what I'm saying.

The same can be true of the *Back to the Future* trilogy, which literally types "To Be Continued" before the ending credits of the first movie. Then, the break at the end of film two requires you to move into the third film, because Marty McFly is stuck in 1955 and Doc Brown is somewhere in the old West. The chase is on.

Look for ways to clearly close book one while leaving subtle hints that book two and three are right around the corner, should you choose to continue to create new problems for the characters and worlds you've created as an author.

If you are planning a sequel, how did you end your first book with a satisfying close?

_____
_____
_____ .

Name 3-5 story threads that you left open that can be picked up and continued in book two.

_____
_____
_____ .

What is your overarching story problem left unresolved that will keep your series going?

_____
_____
_____ .

If you closed all the story threads, or left book one on a cliffhanger, work out how you might make changes to fix those issues here.

_____
_____
_____ .

Chapter Forty-Three:

Falling Action

The final twenty minutes of *The Lord of the Rings: The Return of the King* might have enough plot points to fill an entire fourth film in the series. The ring has been destroyed, Middle Earth has won, and the arduous journey is over. Frodo awakens to his friends from the Shire, and there is fellowship, laughter, and love.

But the story doesn't stop here.

The falling action starts. We head back to the Shire, we talk with Bilbo, he releases his first book, and goes essentially on a book tour. Sam asks out the Hobbit woman of his dreams, they marry, and everyone lives happily ever after, except Frodo, whose price for magic is to leave the Shire he loved so much, forever.

I say every time I see this extended falling action that it could have been stretched into an entire movie. And I don't mean that as a good thing.

Falling action, like the introduction, should be just long enough to close the loose ends of the story. Once the climax peaks, your reader has received the satisfaction they've been waiting for. They don't necessarily want to stick around too much longer. And they definitely don't want to feel like they're stuck turning pages. A great meal with perfect ambiance, food, and service can be ruined if it takes too long to get the bill after dessert.

In *Hunger Games*, the games end, Katniss returns home, and the gamemaker is punished for his choices. She and Peeta share a moment on the train, Katniss sees Gale and Prim, and that pretty much closes things out. Just enough time for the happy-feels to set in, knowing that danger is lurking around the corner, but not today.

My novel *Dreadlands: Wolf Moon* ends in much the same way. The battle is over and Arud wakes up in the city by the sea, meets his uncle, sees that his sister is okay, and has a moment with Scalvia, the girl he falls in love with. His father is missing, the wolves have been quieted, and he knows it's the calm before the storm. But in that moment, the story problem has been resolved and Arud smiles in the peace of the victory, if only till the next battle.

As a writer, you must be careful not to provide too much falling action as well as ripping off the reader with not enough falling action. When a story ends too soon, it can feel rushed and leave the reader with unanswered questions. When it's too long, it can be frustrating. In either case, a wonderful novel can leave a bad taste in your reader's mouth if you don't craft a well-balanced falling action and ending.

And bad taste means bad reviews.

Have you tried to cram an entire book into your falling action? How much of that information is for you, the writer, verses how much of it is necessary for your reader to answer story questions? Do you have another book in the falling action that you can use for a sequel or series? If not, would the information be better served as an epilogue?

Another choice is to let the information sit in the "bonus material" section, like on a DVD, where you can review behind the scenes footage, see hilarious outtakes, or even alternate endings. You can give all those incredible details that you wanted to include in the end of the story as a companion novella or digital short story. Christina Benjamin has published several companion novellas that go into the supporting character's stories. It's a great way to get details to the reader that are cut from the novel because they don't push the story forward.

Another creative way is to take those elements in the extended falling action and slowly trickle them out on social media to build buzz. You can also offer those short pieces as rewards to your Patreon subscribers. The point is you don't have to delete your work in the falling action. Find creative ways to share it with your reader instead.

If you have you tried to cram an entire book into your falling action, where can you break it off?

_____
_____
_____ .

How much of that information is for you, the writer, verses how much of it is necessary for your reader to answer story questions? Explain.

_____
_____
_____ .

Maybe you have another book in the falling action that you can use for a sequel or series. Expand on a premise for a sequel or series.

_____
_____
_____ .

If you don't find enough to create a sequel or series, would the information be better served as an epilogue? Summarize it here.

_____
_____
_____
_____
_____ .

Chapter Forty-Four:

Beyond Main Characters

Even if it's not the main story, every character in your book has a story of their own. Whether or not the reader ever learns about it, every character in your book has their own past, present, and future. When thinking beyond main characters, you open the door for the spinoff series.

There are several different ways to do this successfully. *The Chronicles of Riddick* spinoff from *Pitch Black* was a completely new origin story of the character of Riddick, who was so interesting that audiences needed to know his story. In a spinoff, the story happens in the same universe as the original one, but it's either before or after the first story takes place.

The movie *Creed* is the continuation of Rocky's story through the life of his friend's son, Apollo Creed, who is now a fighter looking for Rocky to train him. It is a great story with tributes to the original classic films and characters. In continuation stories, the universe has continued, and a new character is connected to the characters from the original story.

Fantastic Beasts and Where to Find Them is a spinoff from the wizarding world of *Harry Potter.* Not a sequel, but a prequel, a new element of the world in a new universe with mostly new characters. In a prequel, the main story is told first, but something that happened earlier in the story's timeline is shown after. It usually gives more depth to a secondary character or story element we discovered in the main story or series but didn't have enough screen time to satisfy the reader.

We see similar prequels appearing in the *Star Wars* universe and Tolkien's worlds as we read or watch *The Hobbit* and *The Lord of the Rings* series.

My favorite use of the side story is *Star Wars.* I love how in between the main films, standalone stories about Solo, Jyn Erso, and the Mandalorian keep me in the universe while also providing insight into characters I love and even answer some questions, like why did the Death Star have such an obvious, fatal flaw?

The other series that accomplished this extraordinarily well is both *X-Men* and Marvel's *Avengers.* In X-Men, we get origin stories of Logan and we see Charles and Raven as children, and all the X-Men as teenagers. Marvel's Avengers almost all have standalone stories. The characters are slowly integrated into single films with all of them appearing in the Avengers storyline. I think there are more than 15 films in this series. It's brilliant writing and it mirrors the comics in the sense that you get deep into the side stories and find that these characters all have their own purpose, problem, and plot to discover and share with the reader.

This is the type of characters we should strive to create, those that are so dynamic, so unique that they steal the show and demand a show of their own, all while playing the role we crafted them to play in their original story world. It's not an easy task, but it's one that makes you a great writer.

Have you created complex supporting characters with their own stories, goals, motivations, and fears? Or are they flat and uninteresting, simply there to fill in and aid the hero on his journey? Do they prompt the reader to want to know more? How can you build supporting characters strong enough to support their own story while still knowing their place in the story at hand?

What about world building? Have you created a milieu so incredible that the reader craves more stories set within its boundaries? Through balance, you can create believable worlds and characters that your reader will love so much that they insist you share more once they read The End.

How have you created complex supporting characters with their own stories, goals, motivations, and fears?

_____

_____

_____ .

In what ways can you give purpose to characters who seem to only help the hero on his journey?

_____

_____

_____ .

How can you prompt the reader to want to know more?

_____

_____

_____ .

How can you build supporting characters strong enough to support their own story while still knowing their place in the story at hand?

_____

_____

_____ .

What about world building? Have you created a milieu so incredible that the reader craves more stories set within its boundaries?

_____

_____

_____ .

Author's Note

I hope you found many new ideas to improve your own book. If you want more insight, reach out! I love helping authors and sharing what I've learned in my decade plus of publishing and writing books. I'm also a great speaker (wink, wink) and would love to come out to your conference or school to speak.

Above all, keep writing, keep stretching yourself, and never stop learning how to write a book that doesn't suck!

Up next in this series? Publishing, Selling, and Marketing a Book that doesn't Suck!

wwww.theWRITEengle.com / theWRITEengle@gmail.com

Works Cited

Harry Potter Series
Lord of the Rings
Trilogy
Pinocchio
Legend
Percy Jackson Series
Robin Hood
The Matrix
X-Men
Superman
It's A Wonderful Life
Hunger Games Trilogy
The Wizard of Oz
Indiana Jones
Franchise
Journey to the Center
of the Earth
The Time Machine
Gone with the Wind
The Fault of Our Stars
50 Shades of Gray
Jerry Maguire
Ender's Game
The Chronicles of
Narnia
Star Wars Franchise
Holes
The Lemonade War
Cinder

Beezus and Ramona
Batman
Back to the Future
Trilogy
On Writing
Carrie
Orson Buggy's Big
Fang Theory
Lord of the Flies
Goldilocks and the
Three Bears
Divergent
Rita Hayworth and the
Shawshank
Redemption
The Life of Pi
The Hobbit
300
Rambo
Shrek
Monk
Dumbo
Looper
Pitch Black
Disney
Aladdin
The Lion King
The Princess and the
Frog

Invasion of the Body
Snatchers
The Lottery
Lynnwood
Thinner
The Tell-Tale Heart
The Monkey's Paw
A Christmas Carol
The Maze Runner
Gregor the Overlander
Spiderman
Cinderella
The Man in the Iron
Mask
Twilight
Supernatural
Catching Fire
Revenge of the Sith
Snow White
Romeo and Juliet
The Geneva Project
Breaking Dawn
The Da Vinci Code
Great Expectations
Scooby-Doo Mysteries
The Underland
Chronicles
Gregor and the Curse
of the Warmbloods
The Sixth Sense
How the Grinch Stole
Christmas

The Phantom
Tollbooth
The Chronicles of
Riddick
Greed
Fantastic Beasts and
Where to Find Them
Dreadlands
Clifton Chase and the
Arrow of Light
The Dredge
Stranger Things
Metal Mouth

If you enjoyed this book, please take a moment to review it.

Follow the author on all social media platforms @thewriteengle

Want to support and get free stuff? Join the Tribe: Patreon.com/theWRITEengle

ABOUT THE AUTHOR

Jaimie Engle lives in Melbourne, Florida, with her husband, youngest son, and hound dog. When she isn't making up stories, she's probably making story-scented candles, watching movies, or cosplaying.